THE
White Spot
COOKBOOK

Kerry Gold

THE
White Spot
COOKBOOK

FIGURE 1 PUBLISHING *Vancouver*

Cataloguing data available from Library and Archives Canada
978-0-9918588-7-3

Editing by Lucy Kenward
Copy editing by Iva Cheung
Cover and interior design by Peter Cocking
Food photography by John Sherlock
Food styling by Nathan Fong
Printed and bound in Canada by Friesens
Distributed in Canada by Raincoast
Distributed in the U.S. by Publishers Group West

The photo that appears top row, centre, on page 2,
and on page 28, is courtesy of the Vancouver Public Library 59417.
The photo on page 78 is courtesy of the *Vancouver Sun*.
The image on page 79 is courtesy of Red Robinson.

Figure 1 Publishing Inc.
Vancouver BC Canada
www.figure1pub.com

Contents

A Word of Welcome

WELCOME TO WHITE SPOT's very first cookbook, which is, at heart, a celebration of what we do best—serving the loyal guests who've made us a B.C. institution since 1928.

Young British Columbians might not know that we go back that far, that we were the brainchild of a young, baseball-loving entrepreneur named Nat Bailey. Nat lived life the way it should be lived. He followed his passions, and he had a passion for the restaurant business. Nat started out of a Ford Model T truck and grew White Spot to a thriving operation throughout B.C.

The Toigo family, also B.C.-raised entrepreneurs, is continuing Nat's legacy of warm hospitality, locally sourced fresh food and pioneering spirit. We are a family-run operation, and we treat our guests and staff like family as well. It's a part of our corporate culture that is in daily practice in each of our 120-plus White Spot and Triple-O's restaurants across Western Canada and Asia and in our interactions with the 17 million guests we serve each year. At White Spot, we have unlimited opportunities to make a difference in people's days, and often in their lives.

As owners Peter Jr. and Ron Toigo like to say, we are nothing without our guests. So, as much as we plan to grow, we'll always be true to our roots, delivering on our promise of what you have come to expect from us—our Legendary Burgers with Triple "O" sauce; our fresh-cut fries; our fresh seasonal salads, entrées and desserts; and our cherished Pirate Paks for kids. We understand that the connection our guests have to White Spot is an emotional one—memories of Pirate Paks at the drive-in, all the kids crammed into the backseat; a slice of hot, freshly baked pie on a first date; a frosty, hand-scooped milkshake with friends from school.

In this book, we bring you some of our favourite oldies and our contemporary menu items, too, specially tailored for the home cook by our own chefs. We also bring you some of our favourite moments over the years. Welcome.

WARREN ERHART
President and CEO, White Spot Restaurants

FACING: Entrance to White Spot in North Nanaimo, B.C.

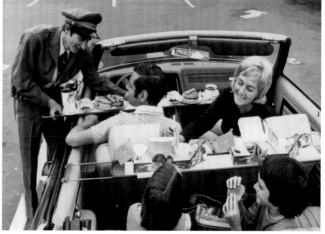

Our Loyalty to Past & Present

B EING CANADA's longest-running restaurant chain is a fair bit of responsibility. For one thing, you can't mess with a legend. There are few restaurants in the world with the history and fierce guest loyalty of White Spot. British Columbians, especially, have grown up with us, so it would be easy to take White Spot for granted, what with 65 full-service restaurants and 64 Triple-O's, including 11 in Asia, where we continue to grow. But we've never taken our own success for granted, which is the key to our longevity. The Toigo family, owners since 1982, understand that survival in the highly competitive restaurant industry means we can never get too comfortable with what we've achieved.

"Most importantly, we always need to pay attention," says Peter Toigo Jr., Managing Director of Shato Holdings, the company that has owned White Spot since 1982. "You have to look after your guests. You have to listen to them, listen to your people." We listen because of that responsibility we feel to both our founder Nat Bailey's legacy and to our guests, who number more than one million a month at our White Spot restaurants alone.

"It's really a unique feeling—you walk down any street, and you'll find someone who's got a White Spot story," says our President, Warren Erhart. "I think all of us feel a responsibility for the brand."

There's the responsibility, and then there's the ongoing need to meet the demands of our new guests—the need for innovation. There have been a lot of firsts throughout our history. We were Canada's first drive-in restaurant. We were sourcing fresh, locally grown ingredients long before there was ever a 100-mile diet or a slow food movement. We popularized fried chicken before anyone had heard of anything Kentucky fried. We led the burger craze of the 1950s before Vancouver had witnessed a pair of golden arches.

If you count our grassroots beginnings, we might even have launched Canada's first food cart. We were pioneers in our field, and we set the evolutionary bar pretty high.

A Boy, His Truck & a Dream

OUR FOUNDER, NAT Bailey, was a young man with a big idea and a lot of drive. Like all great entrepreneurs, he saw beyond the status quo.

When Nat was getting started, in the 1920s, South Vancouver and Point Grey were separate districts that had just joined Vancouver, making it the third-largest city in Canada. Granville Street was a long dirt road that ran across the city to Marpole, where there were more trees than buildings. Vancouver was so new there were still farms and dairies in the city proper. The arrival of the automobile was hugely exciting, even though the only one you could drive was a Ford Model T.

With the emergence of the car, it became a favourite pastime to go for a long drive out to the country. People liked to dress up for their automobile rides. The men wore bowlers, and the ladies dressed in

FACING: Nat Bailey, Founder

Original BBQ staff, 1929. Nat Bailey is on the far right.

long skirts and flapper hats pulled down over their ears. Ever the savvy entrepreneur, Nat saw an opportunity in these carloads of people and capitalized on it by selling peanuts, hot dogs and ice cream out of his Ford Model T truck, which was plastered in menu signage and set up at Lookout Point on Southwest Marine Drive near the University of British Columbia. That was the place to stop and take in the view before you'd head on your way, bouncing down a dirt road in your prized automobile. Nat was a driven kid who was all about work, so it wasn't long before he had his own crew of kids serving hot dogs and soda pops. Nat's truck was probably Canada's first food cart.

With his earnings, Nat purchased some property on the fringes of the city, at 67th Avenue and Granville, and opened a small BBQ chicken shack. He named it White Spot, and on the roof he painted a big white spot. He'd heard the name once before and liked it, and besides, it brought to mind the sort of sparkling clean place you'd want to eat at. He bought more property nearby, and on June 16, 1928, he launched what would become the first official White Spot restaurant.

He built a big, white log cabin restaurant with green trim, the now-legendary but long-gone building that many Vancouverites remember as children. That drive-in became the place to be, and as a result cars were soon lined up along Granville Street. The biggest rush came around 9 p.m., when the movie crowd got out and headed to the Spot.

White Spot wouldn't have looked anything like the modern incarnation. Much of the 1920s was the era of Prohibition, that contradictory time when alcohol was verboten and yet the underground speak-easy was thriving. White Spot was born at the tail end of this crazy period, and at its inception, the menu would have been entirely of the era. People of the '20s replaced any alcohol craving with sugar, which meant intensely sweet desserts, such as moulded Jell-O, pine-apple upside-down cakes, rum cakes flavoured with extract and sweetened with hard sauce, devil's food cake and angel food cake, and maraschino cherries adorning everything. Soft drinks, punch, lemonade, Coca-Cola, ginger ale, Kool-Aid and sweet iced tea were popular drinks. Tea houses were all the rage, with delicate tea sand-wiches and their simple fillings, like ham, chicken salad, egg salad and cream cheese. Popular store-bought brands had entered the mainstream, and kitchen cooks had the help of Campbell's soups,

Canada's First Drive-In

NAT BAILEY was a pioneer who developed not only Canada's first drive-in restaurant but most likely also the world's first drive-in food tray. Instead of using plastic, Nat's first trays were long cedar planks painted white. Nat's business partner, Bob Stout, a former carhop, came up with the idea, and the two men created the result. Bob stayed with White Spot for 50 years, which is even longer than Nat!

The original White Spot BBQ chicken shack at 67th and Granville in Vancouver opened on June 16, 1928.

Aunt Jemima pancake flour, Heinz ketchup, Sanka coffee, Underwood Deviled Ham, Ovaltine and Kellogg's Corn Flakes. For a good many, it was a prosperous time, and although it was certainly not a period of culinary adventure, the people of the 1920s and the early 1930s loved to socialize and indulge in the latest fad.

By 1938, when Nat expanded business with the sit-down Granville Dining Room, his menu included the simple foods of the era, a choice of fruit cocktail or tomato juice, homemade hot biscuits with greengage jam or honey, Delnor fresh frosted peas, and roasted stuffed young tom turkey with cranberry jelly. The dining room became another hit—the place to go for a celebratory meal or a Sunday night dinner. It might have been the Depression, or the "Dirty '30s," but Vancouverites were in the mood to be treated special. Nat's White Spot filled a much-needed void, and our reputation for high-quality food and service started to spread.

FACING: White Spot Dining Room, 1943.

"Girl Hops" were a White Spot mainstay during the war years (early 1940s).

That's not to say it was smooth sailing for Nat and his wife, Eva, who worked at White Spot too. They saw White Spot through the tough times of both the Depression and the Second World War, and they worked a lot of overtime to keep the restaurants going through bleak economic times, supply shortages due to rationing, and understaffing when many young men went off to war. To keep the operation running, Nat hired lots of women, and many of them worked at the commissary located in a building behind the Granville and 67th Avenue location. By 1948, the commissary had grown to 4,000 square feet and was a hub of cooking, baking and prepping using local ingredients delivered by truck from nearby farms throughout the day.

In those days, the pie lineup was the star of the operation: the boysenberry, blueberry, apple, raspberry and strawberry pies were all top sellers. Nat also refused to use any frozen

The Granville Dining Room opened in 1938 and was in its heyday in 1942 despite the war.

FACING: Peter Guichon (centre) with Executive Chef Chuck Currie (left) and Red Seal Chef Jennifer Moyou (right) at White Spot Farms, 2009.

or processed ingredients, and in order to follow his own policy, he bought a parcel of land in Surrey, B.C., and launched Newton Farms to maintain his high standard of chicken production.

Then there were the potatoes. We've been buying potatoes locally since Mr. Bailey shook hands with a potato farmer named Felix Guichon. Because the fries are a beloved White Spot tradition, the potatoes, and where they come from, matter a lot. By 1935, the Guichon family had started a potato co-op, and Nat became a regular customer. Our method of frying those potatoes hasn't changed much since Nat's day. Many modern kitchens use frozen fries because, to be honest, fresh-cut fries are a bit of a hassle. Potatoes have to be scrubbed and cut, of course. And then we fry them. And fry them again, because we want them extra crispy. You can imagine the inconvenience of all that cutting and double frying. But as we said, there's a responsibility that comes with inheriting a legacy.

Not Just Any Spud

THE POTATO co-op disbanded by 1992, but Guichon's Felix Farms, now the biggest potato grower in B.C., continues to supply us with our potatoes. We've kept many partnerships over the years.

"My grandfather and my father both knew Nat," says Peter Guichon, who used to go to White Spot with his parents and four siblings when he "was knee-high to a grasshopper." Somehow, he recalls, all seven of them would cram into their car for a meal at the drive-in.

"Mr. Bailey was a very good man to deal with. He had a vision and he built on it. He talked about it all the time. He believed, and the Toigo family believes today, that the fresh-cut French fries are superior to frozen. We can thank the Toigo family, because a lot of people have tried to convince them to switch to frozen. They're easier to handle. But that family has stuck together and said, 'No, we have a business built on fresh-cut fries.'"

The potato we use these days is the Kennebec, predominantly grown in B.C. It's a white, thin-skinned variety with a distinct flavour. You can't purchase it in a grocery store because it's grown only for commercial use, but it's showing up in restaurant kitchens now that chefs are getting picky about their varieties. While it's a rather plain-looking potato, it's got superior flavour and versatility, which is why we've counted on it for 50 or so years. At one time, we considered switching to a different potato, and we spent lots of time and money testing varieties throughout North America. But we came back to the Kennebec in the end.

Breakfast

Eggs Benedict *14*

Lifestyle Mushroom-Spinach Frittata *15*

Santa Fe Breakfast Burrito *16*

Buttermilk Pancakes & Waffles *19*

Giardino Omelette *20*

Eggs Benedict

SERVES 4

HOLLANDAISE SAUCE

2 Tbsp white wine vinegar

2 shallots, in ¼-inch dice (¼ cup)

¼ tsp coarse black pepper

¼ cup water

4 large egg yolks

½ lb melted unsalted butter (1 cup), cooled slightly

1 Tbsp fresh lemon juice

Pinch of cayenne pepper

⅛ tsp kosher salt

POACHED EGGS

1 tsp kosher salt

2 Tbsp white vinegar

8 large eggs

4 English muffins

8 slices back bacon

THIS RECIPE IS everyone's favourite brunch item. Real hollandaise sauce is worth the trouble and wows your friends and family. Serve with fresh fruit.

HOLLANDAISE SAUCE In a small saucepan on medium heat, combine vinegar, shallots, pepper and water and simmer for about 2 minutes, or until reduced to about 2 Tbsp. Strain ingredients through a fine-mesh sieve into a clean bowl, discarding any solids. Set aside and allow to cool.

Place egg yolks in a stainless steel bowl and whisk until lightly beaten. In a pot just slightly larger in diameter than the bowl, bring about an inch of water to the steaming point on high heat. Set the bowl of egg yolks in the pot, add the vinegar reduction and whisk the two together. In a very slow and steady stream, add the butter, vigorously whisking the mixture using a figure-eight motion and scraping the sides of the bowl until the mixture emulsifies. Remove from the heat when the sauce has thickened enough to form "ribbons" as you whisk. Stir in lemon juice and cayenne. Season with salt. Use within 1 hour.

POACHED EGGS Fill a large frying pan with 1½ to 2 inches of water. Add salt and vinegar and bring to a low simmer on medium-low heat. (Adding vinegar to the water helps the eggs keep their shape rather than dispersing.)

Gently crack eggs, one at a time, into the simmering water. Poach until yolks are medium-firm, exactly 4 minutes. (For firmer yolks or for extra-large or jumbo eggs, poach 4½ minutes; for looser yolks or for medium-sized eggs, poach 3 minutes.) Remove eggs with a slotted spoon, pat dry with paper towel and transfer to a clean plate.

While eggs are poaching, toast English muffins and lightly sauté back bacon. Set 2 halves of an English muffin, cut side up, on each plate. Top each muffin half with a slice of back bacon and a poached egg, then spoon hollandaise sauce overtop.

Mushroom-Spinach Frittata

COMING UP WITH our Lifestyle Choices menu items took four times as long as developing our other recipes. That's because we were determined to have them taste really good, not just be good for you. To make one big frittata, cook the ingredients in a 12-inch nonstick pan, or divide the mixture into four and cook individual servings in a smaller, 7-inch pan. Serve with fresh fruit.

HEAT canola oil in a medium nonstick frying pan on medium-high. Add mushrooms, bell peppers, red onions, salt and pepper and sauté until mushrooms are lightly golden, about 2 minutes. Stir in spinach, cook for 30 seconds, then reduce the heat to medium. Add egg whites all at once, stirring until the mixture starts to set, about 3 minutes. Sprinkle with cheese and cover the pan for 30 to 60 seconds until cheese is melted. Slide the frittata onto a platter and serve immediately.

SERVES 4

2 tsp canola oil

⅓ cup sliced mushrooms (about 4 mushrooms)

1 red bell pepper, in ¼-inch dice (1 cup)

½ red onion, in ¼-inch dice (¾ cup)

⅛ tsp kosher salt

½ tsp coarse black pepper

4 cups spinach leaves, washed and patted dry

2 cups egg whites

¼ cup shredded medium cheddar cheese

Santa Fe Breakfast Burrito

SERVES 4

PICO DE GALLO SALSA

2 tomatoes, in
¼-inch dice (1½ cups)

2 Tbsp drained and diced
canned jalapeño peppers
(or 1 fresh jalapeño pepper,
seeded and diced)

½ onion, in ¼-inch
dice (¾ cup)

¼ bunch cilantro,
finely chopped

1 tsp fresh lime juice

¼ tsp kosher salt

LIME-CILANTRO SOUR CREAM

½ cup sour cream

1 Tbsp chopped
fresh cilantro

1½ Tbsp fresh lime juice

CHICKEN BURRITOS

2 Tbsp butter

4 skinless, boneless
chicken breasts, each
4 oz, in ¼-inch slices

1 onion, in ¼-inch
slices (1½ cups)

1 red bell pepper,
in ¼-inch dice (1 cup)

1 green bell pepper, in
¼-inch dice (1 cup)

2 tsp minced garlic

1 tsp chili powder

1 tsp kosher salt

½ tsp coarse black pepper

½ tsp ground cumin

½ tsp dried whole-
leaf oregano

¼ tsp cayenne pepper

2 tomatoes, seeded,
in ¼-inch strips

8 large eggs

1 cup shredded medium
cheddar cheese

1 cup shredded
Monterey Jack cheese

4 flour tortillas, each
12 inches, warmed
briefly in a 350°F oven

THIS RECIPE MAKES a nice, filling breakfast dish with a Southwestern flavour. For an extra kick, add a dash of your favourite hot sauce to the pico de gallo salsa. The salsa and the sour cream do not keep well, but they're so delicious you're unlikely to have leftovers.

SALSA Combine all ingredients until well mixed.

SOUR CREAM Combine all ingredients until well mixed.

CHICKEN BURRITOS Heat butter in a large frying pan on medium-high. Add chicken, onions, bell peppers, garlic and spices and cook for about 8 minutes, or until chicken is just cooked but still juicy. Stir in tomatoes, eggs and cheeses and cook, stirring until eggs are just set and cheese is just melted, 2 to 3 minutes.

Divide the filling among the tortillas, placing it in an 8-inch by 2-inch line across the middle. Fold the sides of the tortilla over the filling and then, starting from the bottom, roll up the tortilla. Be sure to roll tightly so that the burrito is firm and the filling can't escape. If necessary, secure each end of the burrito with a toothpick. Serve immediately on individual plates, topped with pico de gallo salsa and lime-cilantro sour cream.

Buttermilk Pancakes & Waffles

THE SAME RECIPE works well for both. For a special treat, try a little demerara or brown sugar and freshly squeezed lemon juice sprinkled over your cakes or waffles instead of the usual maple syrup and butter. You will be delighted!

STRAWBERRY TOPPING In a large bowl, toss strawberries with sugar. Allow to sit, tossing occasionally, for 30 minutes. In a food processor, purée half of the berries until smooth, then combine with the remaining berries.

PANCAKES OR WAFFLES Combine flours, sugar, salt, baking powder and baking soda in a large bowl. In a separate bowl, whisk together buttermilk, butter, eggs, sour cream and vanilla until well mixed. Add the buttermilk mixture to the dry ingredients and stir until just combined. Allow the mixture to rest at room temperature for 15 minutes.

Heat a large nonstick frying pan or waffle iron on medium. Add a dab of butter to the pan (or lightly grease the waffle iron with cooking spray). Ladle ⅓ cup of batter into the pan (or ¾ cup onto a large waffle iron) and cook for 2 minutes per side for pancakes (or 4 minutes in the waffle iron). Repeat with the remaining batter. To serve, top waffles or pancakes with strawberry topping.

SERVES 4
(Makes 8 pancakes
or 4 large waffles)

STRAWBERRY TOPPING
1 lb strawberries, quartered

¼ cup granulated sugar

PANCAKES OR WAFFLES
1½ cups all-purpose flour

1½ cups cake flour

1½ Tbsp granulated sugar

1 tsp kosher salt

1½ tsp baking powder

¾ tsp baking soda

2 cups buttermilk

¼ cup melted butter
+ more for greasing the pan

3 large eggs

¼ cup sour cream

½ tsp vanilla extract

Giardino Omelette

SERVES 4

ARRABBIATA SAUCE

1 Tbsp extra-virgin olive oil

½ onion, in ¼-inch dice (¾ cup)

2 tsp minced garlic

½ tsp kosher salt

¼ tsp coarse black pepper

Pinch of crushed chilies

⅛ tsp cayenne pepper

Dash of Tabasco sauce

1 can (14 fl oz/398 mL) tomatoes, chopped but not drained

1 Tbsp chopped fresh basil leaves

Pinch of granulated sugar

1 Tbsp grated Italian parmesan cheese

GIARDINO OMELETTE

12 large eggs

2 Tbsp milk

1¾ tsp kosher salt

½ tsp white pepper

1 green bell pepper, in ¼-inch dice (1 cup)

¾ cup sliced mushrooms

6 green onions, in ⅛-inch slices (¾ cup)

1 tomato, in ¼-inch dice (¾ cup)

¼ medium zucchini, in ¼-inch dice (1 cup)

¾ tsp coarse black pepper

2 Tbsp butter

1 cup spinach leaves

¾ cup mixed shredded medium cheddar and mozzarella cheese

THE NAME SAYS it all: an Italian "garden" omelette that's delicious even if you're not vegetarian. Serve your omelette with the optional arrabbiata sauce if you like your eggs spicy.

ARRABBIATA SAUCE Heat olive oil in a small saucepan on medium. Add onions, garlic, spices and Tabasco sauce and cook until onions are just translucent, about 5 minutes. Stir in tomatoes and simmer, covered, for 10 minutes. Remove from the heat and stir in basil, sugar and parmesan.

GIARDINO OMELETTE Whisk together eggs, milk, 1 tsp of the salt and white pepper. Combine vegetables (except the spinach) in a large bowl and season with the remaining ¾ tsp of salt and black pepper.

Melt butter in a large frying pan on high heat. Add ¼ of the vegetable mixture and sauté until vegetables are just softened and mushrooms are golden, about 3 minutes. Ladle ¼ of the egg mixture (¾ cup) over the vegetables and add ¼ of the spinach. Stir vigorously and continuously until eggs are 80 per cent cooked, then stop and allow eggs to set. Cook for 15 seconds, then flip omelette over to cook the other side. Sprinkle ¼ of the cheese over the middle of the omelette and cook for 15 more seconds. Roll up the omelette, enclosing the cheese, and transfer to a serving plate. Repeat with the remaining vegetables, eggs and cheese until you have 4 omelettes. Pour ¼ cup of arrabbiata sauce over each omelette and serve immediately.

Let's Go to
the Spot

WHITE SPOT HAD survived, and even thrived, during its first 20 years, but the 1950s was the beginning of a period that belonged to the saddle-shoe- and poodle-skirt-wearing teenager, and a huge part of that subculture involved burgers, drive-ins and soda fountains. White Spot was at the epicentre of it all, and every night at any of our drive-ins was like a scene from TV's *Happy Days*.

In those early days, we were more known for chicken than burgers, if you can believe it, but the whole world was celebrating the burger, and again, thanks to Nat, we were the trendsetter. Our biggest sellers were comfort-food classics, including our famous Chicken Pick'ns and Chicken in the Straw, which was four pieces of our Chicken Pick'ns served on a basket of our famous fries. Our version of fried chicken had a slightly sweet batter—served up with a side of our thick-cut fries,

FACING: The second White Spot location was on Burrard Street near the Hotel Vancouver. It opened in 1948 and would become the first of our restaurants to offer breakfast.

crispy on the outside, piping hot potato-ey goodness on the inside. And, of course, our burgers. Just like today, we combined a grilled patty made of 100 per cent fresh Canadian grade-A, double-ground chuck, served on a toasted artisan-style bun. Nat had the custom bun baked with a horizontal grain to keep our signature secret Triple "O" sauce—which derived its name from the "OOO" abbreviation used by carhops to indicate extra toppings—from soaking through, and the bun was so fresh that it had to air out for a couple of hours before the kitchen crew could properly slice it. And the burgers were finished with the trademark slice of dill pickle laid across the top of the bun. Back then, the burger was sliced in half, like a sandwich, so when you picked it up you'd see all the layers of meat, cheese, and Triple "O" sauce.

Business was booming, and it showed no signs of slowing down. Erwin Jellen, who started with us as a dishwasher in 1953 at the now long-gone White Spot drive-in at 850 Burrard Street, recalls that

Carhop in the famous peaked cap at the Broadway and Larch location in Vancouver, c. 1950s.

the hot rods would be lined up all the way down Burrard Street, to St. Paul's Hospital. Once they made it inside the drive-in, the kids would order the 45-cent burgers and 20-cent side of fries. In those days, the drive-in was open until 2 a.m., so it was quite the scene. "You always wanted to get the back-end spot because then you could see who was cruising by," adds broadcaster Wayne Cox, who started coming to our restaurants as a kid and still comes today. "There were no cellphones, so you had to keep up with the action by actually talking to people."

By 1955, Nat had opened his new Park Royal Drive-in and Coffee Shop to much fanfare in what was one of Canada's largest shopping malls at the time. He also expanded the Granville Street Dining Room and launched a $250,000 dining room at the new Oakridge Shopping Centre. He opened locations in Victoria, in New Westminster and at Southeast Marine in Vancouver. And he purchased ICL Catering, a catering and events company. A natural speaker and

White Spot's 25th-Anniversary menu included a personal message of thanks from Eva and Nat to their guests.

A Purple Hot Rod and a Burger

LEGENDARY MUSIC manager Bruce Allen has been going to White Spot since he was a kid growing up in Vancouver. But the White Spot highlight for Bruce was his teenage years, when he discovered the dream of the drive-in and car culture. Bruce had been counting the days until he could get a driver's licence, just so that he could pull into our drive-in at 67th and Granville.

"There'd be a lineup of kids along Granville Street to get a spot at that drive-in. We'd sit there for about 45 minutes. Drive-ins in those days were hangouts, and that was the big one," says Bruce. "Everybody was there with their hot cars and their dates, listening to the radio, standing around talking. It was like going to the skating rink or a dance. You just had to go to White Spot. I must have burned up gallons and gallons of gas idling to get a hamburger."

Bruce was just out of school, and he got a job welding trucks. To say he was proud of his 1950 Monarch was putting it mildly. He'd had it painted just the right purple, with 12 coats of lacquer paint. The interior was a lighter shade of purple, to match. He beefed up the motor and had the chassis lowered. "Boom. Four guys in the car, and off you went to White Spot."

leader, he helped found the Canadian Restaurant Association and was a member of the American Restaurant Association. A diehard baseball fan, in 1956 he co-purchased a triple-A baseball team called the Vancouver Mounties.

By the late 1950s, Nat had taken on five partners who'd been long-time employees: Art Jones, Cecil Eustace, Ernie Creamer, Roy Parkinson and Bob Stout. While Nat acted as President, his partners ran the day-to-day operations. At the time, White Spot had a staff of about 350 working at six locations. With his grandsons along for the ride, Nat would roll into one of his drive-ins, trying to act like a customer. Of course, the staff all knew Nat and instantly recognized him. "I was weaned on Triple 'O' sauce," recalls Mark Andrews, one of Nat's grandsons who was raised by his grandfather and took turns with his brother sampling the food during these all-day inspections. "I could only do two; I'd get so full. Papa Nat would point out all the little things—if the tray wasn't set up properly, the creaminess of the ice cream and the quality of the burgers." However grassroots his approach, he had instituted a way of maintaining standards, which we continue to this day.

Joe Scianna is one of our longest-serving employees. In 1951, at 13 years old, he had arrived with his family from Sicily and was keen to work at Vancouver's hottest hangout. He remembers he met with Nat, who found Joe an Italian-speaking employee to help him fill out the application. He told Joe, "I have no job for you now, but tomorrow I might, because one guy is planning to quit." Joe took the bus home to his east side house, and by the time he got there, he had a phone call from Mr. Bailey, who offered him a job as a dishwasher. Within days, Joe went from washing dishes to making coffee and milkshakes, and slicing pies and topping them with soft ice cream. He started at 75 cents an hour. Experienced staff were paid $1 an hour, and Joe knew he'd be earning that if he worked hard. He was a quick study, and by 1959 he was opening restaurants and training kitchen staff. Over the course of his almost 40-year career with us, he opened 76 White Spot locations throughout B.C. Joe retired in 2002, but since then he's graciously returned to open four more restaurants for us when we've needed his expertise.

"And if they want me to come back and open another one, I'll do it," he says, seated in a booth at the White Spot on Marine Drive, the first restaurant he opened.

The Park Royal Dining Room in West Vancouver, c. 1950s.

Joe remembers the big sellers back in those days. The clubhouse, stacked high with turkey roasted at the commissary, crisp bacon and locally grown tomatoes. Toasted shrimp sandwiches, packed with sweet fresh shrimp and tangy mayo—still a big seller. Of course, the chicken. "Everybody ordered the Chicken Pick'ns," recalls Joe. Even today, our long-time guests still ask for it. The other old-school classics included barbecued beef and barbecued roast chicken on a bun. The strawberry shortcake and boysenberry pie were regulars on those narrow trays that the carhops somehow carried, two at a time, one tray held high, the other held low.

The drive-in service accounted for about 80 per cent of business, so not a detail was overlooked. Dressed in policeman-style caps, white shirts, ties and dress pants with a stripe down the leg, the carhops would slide the long trays through the window of the car, and the tray would rest on the glass edge of the windows. It was a balancing act, carrying those food-laden trays. For a time, there were even female carhops on roller skates, as was all the rage in

LEFT: Balancing one of Nat's innovative aluminum trays, lightening the load compared with the original wooden trays, c. 1950s.

RIGHT: Nat insisted on quality and regularly visited his restaurants to ensure his high standards were maintained, c. 1955.

Fastest Slicer in the West

OUR VETERAN employee Joe Scianna became our go-to manager for training our kitchen staff because he had clocked so many hours working in the kitchen himself. Joe started with us in 1951, and one of Joe's most talked-about skills was his ability to slice the hamburger buns. Back then, the buns would come in freshly baked and in need of slicing. Burgers were our top seller, as they are now, so it was a job that required a level of dexterity and speed.

The staff would start their day by slicing 600 to 700 buns, then the potatoes. Joe, Erwin Jellen and Frank Krische, who were all grill men at the time, would have bun-slicing competitions, speed-slicing their way through a huge stack of buns. Joe would always win, slicing around 100 buns in less than three minutes. Nobody could beat Joe. "He was always bragging about being the fastest," says Erwin, with a chuckle.

the 1950s. Luckily for the servers, though, that fad didn't last long. Food balanced on trays carried by servers on roller skates—you can imagine the number of potential mishaps. Wayne Cox remembers, "Invariably someone would take the vinegar bottle off one end of the tray and throw the balance off completely. And down the tray would come, tipping forward or backward, and everything would fly everywhere. The poor carhop."

At that time Kentucky Fried Chicken was in its early years, and Nat and his partners were offered the chance to own the franchise for B.C. Although Nat was concerned that the Colonel's chicken would compete with our Chicken Pick'ns, his partners convinced him it was a different enough product that it would be a worthwhile side-business. They formed a separate company, and Nat's partner, Ernie, helmed the KFC operation, which, in B.C., was called Ernie's Fine Foods. When they launched the first three KFC franchises, the Colonel came to B.C. to meet his new business partners.

Al Hewlett, one of our long-time employees, recalls meeting Colonel Sanders, "He was a real southern gentleman. He was wearing a white suit, a string tie, the cane, the goatee. Everything you'd expect. And he kissed the ladies' hands." Al remembers that, unlike the Colonel's other franchisees, Nat and his partners used their own version of potato salad, macaroni salad, coleslaw and biscuits for the KFC in those days. "And the Colonel approved," says Al.

Appetizers & Salads

Caramelized Onion Dip *32*

Bruschetta Pizza *35*

Spicy Italian Sausage Pizza *36*

Pollo Basilico Pizza *37*

Poutine *38*

Butter Lettuce, Cambozola & Almond Salad *41*

Candied Salmon Spinach Salad *42*

Caesar Salad *44*

Santorini Chicken Salad *45*

Caprese Chicken Salad *47*

Lifestyle Asian Chicken Salad *48*

Caramelized Onion Dip

SERVES 4

4 shallots, in ¼-inch slices (½ cup)

1 onion, in ¼-inch dice (1½ cups)

1 Tbsp extra-virgin olive oil

½ tsp kosher salt

¼ tsp coarse black pepper

½ cup cream cheese

½ cup shredded mozzarella cheese

¼ cup grated Italian parmesan cheese

2 Tbsp mayonnaise

½ cup sour cream

2 green onions, roughly chopped (¼ cup)

1½ tsp grainy Dijon mustard

¼ tsp Worcestershire sauce

1½ tsp Tabasco sauce

1 Tbsp chopped fresh parsley

THIS ONION DIP has fantastic flavour! Make peeling onions easier by cutting them in half first from the root to the stem and trimming off the ends. Then just grasp a corner of the onion skin and peel off a layer or two.

Serve this dip warm with tortilla chips, potato chips or pita chips on the side.

PREHEAT THE OVEN to 450 °F. Line a baking sheet with aluminum foil. Arrange shallots and onions in a single layer on the foil-lined baking sheet. Drizzle with olive oil and season with ¼ tsp of the salt and pepper and roast until dark golden brown, about 15 minutes. Allow to cool.

In a food processor, combine roasted shallots and onions with the remaining ingredients and process until mostly smooth but with small chunks of onions and shallots. Warm in the microwave before serving.

Bruschetta Pizza

THIS APPETIZER PAYS tribute to 2008 Canadian Culinary Champion Melissa Craig's love for a simple pizza without tomato sauce but with a little hint of spiciness. Cook the pizzas on a perforated pizza pan or directly on the rack in the oven.

BRUSCHETTA Preheat your barbecue to high heat. Using a pastry brush or your fingers, barely coat bell pepper with olive oil. Place bell pepper on the barbecue and grill, turning it occasionally, until skin is ½ to ¾ blackened and blistered. Remove from the heat and allow pepper to cool to room temperature, about 10 minutes.

We like the flavour and colour of the blackened skin, but peel and discard the skin if you don't. Cut pepper in half, reserving the juice but discarding the stem. Cut pepper, including the membranes and seeds, in ¼-inch dice and place in a bowl with the reserved juice. Add the remaining bruschetta ingredients and mix well with a rubber spatula. Refrigerate until needed.

CHILI OIL Heat olive oil in a small saucepan on medium. Add garlic and chilies and sauté until garlic is light brown, about 3 minutes. Set aside to cool.

BRUSCHETTA PIZZAS Preheat the oven to 450 ° F. Dress pizza crusts with chili oil, then top with cheese, bruschetta, bacon and tomatoes. Season with salt and pepper. Bake until the bruschetta is hot, the crust is crispy and the cheese is fully melted, 10 to 12 minutes. Sprinkle each pizza with parsley. Cut into slices and serve immediately.

SERVES 4

BRUSCHETTA

1 red bell pepper

2 Tbsp extra-virgin olive oil + more for brushing bell pepper

½ tsp minced garlic

½ red onion, in ¼-inch dice (¾ cup)

2 vine-ripened tomatoes, in ¼-inch dice (1½ cups)

½ tsp kosher salt

¼ tsp coarse black pepper

¼ tsp cayenne pepper

¼ tsp Tabasco sauce

1 Tbsp balsamic vinegar

½ cup finely chopped fresh basil leaves

CHILI OIL

¼ cup extra-virgin olive oil

1½ tsp minced garlic

½ tsp crushed chilies

BRUSCHETTA PIZZAS

4 pre-cooked pizza crusts, each 8 inches

1 cup shredded mozzarella cheese

4 slices bacon, cooked crisp, in ½-inch pieces

4 large cherry tomatoes, each in 6 wedges

½ tsp kosher salt

½ tsp coarse black pepper

2 Tbsp chopped fresh parsley

Spicy Italian Sausage Pizza

SERVES 4

4 pre-cooked pizza crusts, each 8 inches

1 cup (1 recipe) Arrabbiata Sauce (page 20)

1 cup shredded mozzarella cheese

2 Tbsp grated Italian parmesan cheese

4 slices back bacon, in ⅛-inch strips

24 thin slices pepperoni sausage

6 slices bacon, cooked crisp, in ½-inch pieces

2 fresh Calabrian sausages, casings removed, sautéed until just cooked, then drained and crumbled

¼ to ⅓ red onion, in ¼-inch dice (⅓ cup)

2 Tbsp finely chopped fresh parsley

PINO POSTERARO is the owner of Cioppino's Mediterranean Grill and Enoteca in Vancouver, and as part of our Celebrity Chefs campaign, we developed this dish with him. Cook the pizzas in a perforated pizza pan or directly on the rack in the oven.

PREHEAT the oven to 450 °F. Dress pizza crusts with arrabbiata sauce, then top with the cheeses and meats. Bake until the meats are hot, the crust is crispy and the cheese is melted, 10 to 12 minutes. Sprinkle each pizza with red onions and parsley. Cut into slices and serve immediately.

Pollo Basilico Pizza

I<small>N ITALIAN,</small> *pollo* means "chicken" and *basilico* means "basil." This is a classic pizza pairing better known as pesto chicken in North America. Cook the pizza in a perforated pizza pan or directly on the rack in the oven.

PESTO In a food processor, purée all ingredients until smooth. Will keep refrigerated in an airtight container or a squeeze bottle for up to 3 days.

POLLO BASILICO PIZZAS Preheat the oven to 400°F. Brush chicken with ½ Tbsp of the butter and season with ⅛ tsp of the salt the and ⅛ tsp of the pepper. Place in a pan and roast until just cooked through, about 15 minutes. Set aside. Increase the oven temperature to 450°F.

Heat the remaining 3 Tbsp butter in a frying pan on medium. Add mushrooms, bell peppers and red onions, season with the remaining ⅛ tsp salt and ⅛ tsp pepper. Sauté lightly until mushrooms are golden, about 5 minutes. Set aside.

Cut chicken into ¼-inch slices. Dress pizza crusts with arrabbiata sauce, then top with chicken, then cheese and finally sautéed vegetables. Bake until the veggies are steaming hot, the crust is crispy and the cheese is fully melted, about 10 to 12 minutes. Squiggle the pesto over the pizzas in nice lines, cut into slices and serve immediately.

SERVES 4

PESTO

1 Tbsp pine nuts

2 Tbsp grated Italian parmesan cheese

2 tsp minced garlic

1 tsp fresh lemon juice

½ tsp coarse black pepper

½ cup extra-virgin olive oil

2 cups fresh basil leaves

POLLO BASILICO PIZZAS

2 skinless, boneless chicken breasts, each 4 oz

3½ Tbsp melted butter

¼ tsp kosher salt

¼ tsp coarse black pepper

1 cup sliced mushrooms

½ red bell pepper, in ¼-inch dice (½ cup)

½ green bell pepper, in ¼-inch dice (½ cup)

¼ to ½ red onion, in ¼-inch dice (⅓ cup)

4 pre-cooked pizza crusts, each 8 inches

1 cup (1 recipe) Arrabbiata Sauce (page 20)

1 cup shredded mozzarella cheese

Poutine

SERVES 4

BEEF GRAVY
3 Tbsp unsalted butter

½ onion, in ½-inch dice (¾ cup)

1 carrot, in ½-inch dice (½ cup)

1 celery stalk, in ½-inch dice (½ cup)

¼ cup all-purpose flour

4 cups beef stock

1 bay leaf

¼ tsp dried thyme

1 tsp kosher salt

½ tsp coarse black pepper

FRENCH FRIES
4 medium russet potatoes, washed, dried and cut in ½-inch strips

1½ Tbsp canola oil

2 tsp kosher salt

12 oz fresh cheese curds

WE LIKE OUR French fries crispy and rustic. The secret to crispy potatoes is to dry them very well, and though you can peel them first, we leave the skins on. Although we use Kennebec potatoes, which are grown only for commercial use, for our fries, you can use russets at home. Have the beef gravy simmering on low while you make the fries.

BEEF GRAVY Heat butter in large heavy-bottomed saucepan on medium. When the foaming subsides, add onions, carrots and celery and cook, stirring frequently, until softened, well browned and slightly syrupy, 40 minutes to 1 hour.

Stir in flour and cook, stirring constantly, until thoroughly browned and fragrant, about 5 minutes. Whisking constantly, gradually add beef stock. Bring to a boil, skimming off any foam that forms on the surface. Reduce the heat to medium-low, add bay leaf, thyme, salt and pepper and simmer, stirring occasionally, until thickened and reduced to 3 cups, 20 to 25 minutes.

Place a fine-mesh strainer over a clean bowl. Strain the gravy, pressing on the solids to extract as much liquid as possible. Discard the solids, and refrigerate gravy for up to 4 days.

FRENCH FRIES Preheat the oven to 450 °F. Place potatoes in a large bowl, add canola oil and salt and mix with your hands or a rubber spatula until well coated. Arrange potatoes in a single layer on a baking sheet and bake for 20 minutes. Using a metal lifter, turn fries over and bake for another 10 minutes.

Divide fries among 4 bowls and top each serving with ¼ of the cheese curds. Pour hot gravy over the cheese. Serve immediately.

Butter Lettuce, Cambozola & Almond Salad

THIS SIMPLE AND delicious salad, featuring Cambozola, a blend of Camembert and blue cheese, can be varied simply by changing the type of vinegar in the dressing. You will have about ¼ cup of vinaigrette.

BASIC VINAIGRETTE In a food processor, purée all ingredients until well mixed and onions and parsley are chopped into small flecks. Will keep refrigerated up to 5 days.

CAMBOZOLA SALAD Line individual salad bowls with butter lettuce leaves like beautiful flowers. Drizzle with 2 Tbsp vinaigrette.

Arrange cheese slices on waxed paper and microwave for just 5 to 10 seconds to soften but not quite melt them. Drape cheese over the lettuce and sprinkle with toasted almonds. Serve immediately.

SERVES 4

BASIC VINAIGRETTE

¾ cup canola or grapeseed oil

½ cup vinegar (we like Champagne, raspberry or sherry)

¼ to ½ red onion, in ¼-inch dice (⅓ cup)

1 Tbsp liquid honey

2 tsp grainy Dijon mustard

½ cup fresh parsley

1½ tsp kosher salt

¾ tsp coarse black pepper

CAMBOZOLA SALAD

2 heads butter lettuce, leaves washed and patted dry with paper towel

8 oz Cambozola cheese, thinly sliced

¼ cup sliced almonds, toasted

Candied Salmon Spinach Salad

SERVES 4

CHAMPAGNE VINAIGRETTE

¾ cup Champagne vinegar

½ red onion, in ½-inch dice (¾ cup)

2 Tbsp liquid honey

4 tsp grainy Dijon mustard

¾ cup fresh parsley

1 Tbsp kosher salt

1½ tsp coarse black pepper

1½ cups canola or grapeseed oil

GINGERED PECANS

1 Tbsp granulated sugar

1 large egg white

½ tsp finely grated fresh ginger

Pinch of cinnamon

1 cup pecan halves

SPINACH SALAD

12 oz spinach leaves, washed and patted dry

8 large strawberries, quartered

1 cup blueberries

½ red onion, in ½-inch dice (¾ cup)

½ cup crumbled goat's cheese

1 cup candied salmon, in ¼-inch strips

THIS DISH WAS developed for our Celebrate BC promotion, in which we feature fresh, local ingredients, such as fresh blueberries from local farms, candied salmon from a small producer in Port Hardy and goat's cheese from a dairy in the Okanagan.

CHAMPAGNE VINAIGRETTE Combine all ingredients in a food processor and purée until parsley and onions are in small flecks. Will keep refrigerated for up to 5 days.

GINGERED PECANS Preheat the oven to 350 °F. Line a baking sheet with parchment paper.

Whisk together sugar, egg white, ginger and cinnamon, then add pecans, tossing until well coated. Arrange on the baking sheet and bake for about 7 minutes, stirring once or twice to separate the clusters, until pecans are golden and just fragrant and the glaze has adhered to the nuts. Allow to cool to room temperature, then break nuts apart by crumpling them in the parchment paper. Will keep at room temperature for up to 7 days.

SPINACH SALAD In a large bowl, toss spinach with the Champagne vinaigrette, then divide among 4 plates. Top evenly with the strawberries, blueberries, onions, goat's cheese, salmon and pecans.

Caesar Salad

SERVES 4

CROUTONS

8 thick slices day-old French bread, in 1-inch cubes

2 Tbsp melted unsalted butter

2 Tbsp extra-virgin olive oil

1 tsp chopped fresh oregano leaves

1 tsp chopped fresh thyme leaves

1 tsp minced garlic

CAESAR DRESSING

1 large egg yolk

1 tsp anchovy paste

1 Tbsp minced garlic

1½ tsp grainy Dijon mustard

⅛ tsp Tabasco sauce

¾ tsp Worcestershire sauce

¾ tsp coarse black pepper

½ tsp kosher salt

⅓ cup canola oil

3 Tbsp extra-virgin olive oil

1½ Tbsp fresh lemon juice

1½ tsp red wine vinegar

¼ cup grated Italian parmesan cheese

CAESAR SALAD

2 heads hearts of romaine, washed, spun dry and chopped in 1½-inch pieces

½ cup grated Italian parmesan cheese

4 lemon wedges

A CLASSIC WAY TO start any meal! Homemade croutons are always best, but if you're short on time, good-quality store-bought croutons can be substituted instead.

CROUTONS Preheat the oven to 350° F. Toss together ingredients and arrange in a single layer in a baking pan. Toast until croutons are crispy golden brown, about 10 minutes.

CAESAR DRESSING Place egg yolk, anchovy paste, garlic, mustard, Tabasco sauce, Worcestershire sauce, pepper and salt in a mixer or in a food processor and whip at high speed until well combined. With the motor running, slowly drizzle in canola and olive oils until thickened and emulsified. Stir in lemon juice, vinegar and parmesan.

CAESAR SALAD In a large bowl, toss lettuce with the croutons and dressing, coating the lettuce well. Arrange in a serving bowl and garnish with parmesan and lemon wedges. Serve immediately.

Santorini Chicken Salad

THE LEMON GRILLING sauce for the chicken works well with Greek-inspired dishes and is a perfect match for this salad, which was developed with Melissa Craig, Executive Chef of Bearfoot Bistro in Whistler.

ROASTED SHALLOT VINAIGRETTE Preheat the oven to 350 °F. Lightly brush shallot with olive oil, then place in a roasting pan and cook for about 15 minutes until dark golden brown. Allow to cool. Combine all ingredients in a food processor and purée until smooth. Will keep refrigerated for up to 5 days.

CHICKEN SALAD Preheat the barbecue to medium. Brush chicken breasts with lemon grilling sauce and place them on the grill. Rotate chicken breasts after a minute so that they don't stick and so that they become marked with nice crossed grill marks. Flip the chicken after 4 minutes, and cook for another 4 minutes, rotating the meat on the grill. To test for doneness, poke along the grain with your tongs at the thickest point. The juices should run clear and the meat should be opaque. (If you have a meat thermometer, the internal temperature should read at least 165 °F.)

In a large bowl, toss greens, bell peppers, cucumbers and red onions with the vinaigrette, then divide among 4 plates.

Slice each chicken breast at an angle along its length, creating 3 long strips. Arrange these strips in a fan across the centre of each salad. Top with tomatoes and feta and serve with a slice of pita bread.

SERVES 4

ROASTED SHALLOT VINAIGRETTE

1 large shallot, peeled

3 Tbsp extra-virgin olive oil + more for brushing shallot

2 Tbsp sherry vinegar

2 tsp liquid honey

1 tsp fresh lemon juice

1 tsp minced garlic

¼ tsp dried whole-leaf thyme

¼ tsp kosher salt

⅛ tsp coarse black pepper

Pinch of cayenne pepper

CHICKEN SALAD

4 skinless, boneless chicken breasts, each 4 oz

2½ Tbsp (1 recipe) Lemon Grilling Sauce (page 68)

2 hearts romaine lettuce, in bite-sized pieces

1 radicchio, stemmed, quartered and cut in ⅛-inch slices

2 cups baby arugula (about 1 large handful)

1 red bell pepper, in ½-inch dice (1 cup)

⅓ English cucumber, in ½-inch dice (¾ cup)

½ red onion, in ½-inch dice (¾ cup)

8 large cherry or strawberry tomatoes, halved

½ cup crumbled goat's milk feta cheese

4 rounds pita bread, lightly brushed with extra-virgin olive oil and toasted

Caprese
Chicken Salad

THIS SIMPLE ITALIAN salad made with fresh mozzarella, tomatoes and basil is often served as an antipasto. It's one that Pino Posteraro, owner of Cioppino's Mediterranean Grill and Enoteca, considers one of his favourites. With his input, we turned this dish into an entrée salad by adding chicken and crisp greens. Serve with garlic bread or focaccia.

BASIL VINAIGRETTE Combine all ingredients in a food processor and purée until basil is in small flecks, about 30 seconds. Will keep refrigerated for up to 5 days.

CAPRESE CHICKEN SALAD Preheat the barbecue to medium and the oven to 400°F. Line a baking sheet with parchment paper, arrange prosciutto on top and bake until nicely crisp, 8 to 10 minutes. Set aside.

To make balsamic glaze, heat vinegar in a small saucepan on low heat and simmer until reduced to 4 tsp, about 10 minutes. (You will know it is ready when the mixture simmers in small, thick bubbles rather than large, liquid bubbles.) Set aside.

Brush chicken breasts with lemon grilling sauce and place them on the grill. Rotate chicken breasts after a minute so that they don't stick and so that they become marked with nice crossed grill marks. Flip the chicken after 4 minutes, and cook for another 4 minutes, rotating the meat on the grill. To test for doneness, poke along the grain with your tongs at the thickest point. The juices should run clear and the meat should be opaque. (If you have a meat thermometer, the internal temperature should read at least 165°F.)

In a large bowl, toss greens with the basil vinaigrette, then divide among 4 plates. Slice each chicken breast at an angle along its length, creating 3 long strips. Arrange these strips in a fan across the centre of each salad. Top with tomatoes and bocconcini. Drizzle with balsamic glaze and top with a prosciutto crisp.

SERVES 4

BASIL VINAIGRETTE

2 Tbsp white balsamic vinegar

1 Tbsp finely diced red onions

¼ tsp fresh lemon juice

1¼ tsp liquid honey

2 cups fresh basil leaves

½ tsp grainy Dijon mustard

¼ tsp kosher salt

⅛ tsp coarse black pepper

¼ cup canola oil

CAPRESE CHICKEN SALAD

4 very thin slices prosciutto

¼ cup balsamic vinegar

4 skinless, boneless chicken breasts, each 4 oz

2½ Tbsp (1 recipe) Lemon Grilling Sauce (page 68)

1 heart romaine or leaf lettuce, in bite-sized pieces

1 radicchio, stemmed, quartered and cut in ⅛-inch slices

2 cups baby arugula

8 large cherry or strawberry tomatoes, halved

20 balls baby bocconcini cheese

Asian Chicken Salad

SERVES 4

SOY-GINGER DRESSING

2 Tbsp rice vinegar

2 Tbsp low-sodium soy sauce

1 Tbsp liquid honey

1 tsp minced garlic

1 tsp finely grated fresh ginger

1 tsp finely chopped fresh cilantro

1 green onion, in ⅛-inch diagonal slices (⅛ cup)

¼ tsp sambal oelek

1 tsp sesame oil

ASIAN CHICKEN SALAD

1 cup shelled edamame beans

4 skinless, boneless chicken breasts, each 4 oz

1 tsp Chinese 5-spice powder

2 hearts romaine lettuce, in bite-sized pieces

½ red onion, in ¼-inch dice (¾ cup)

1 red bell pepper, in ½-inch dice (1 cup)

½ celery stalk, in ¼-inch diagonal slices (¼ cup)

2 Tbsp sliced almonds, toasted

THIS POPULAR SALAD was developed for the Lifestyle Choices section of our menu. It's good for you and great tasting too! Find sambal oelek, a puréed Indonesian hot pepper sauce, at Asian markets or your local grocery store.

SOY-GINGER DRESSING Whisk together all ingredients until well combined.

ASIAN CHICKEN SALAD Preheat the barbecue to medium. In a resealable plastic bag, combine edamame with ¼ cup water and microwave for 1 minute. Drain edamame and refrigerate to chill the beans.

Sprinkle chicken breasts with 5-spice powder and place them on the grill. Rotate chicken breasts after a minute so that they don't stick and so that they become marked with nice crossed grill marks. Flip the chicken after 4 minutes, and cook for another 4 minutes, rotating the meat on the grill. To test for doneness, poke along the grain with your tongs at the thickest point. The juices should run clear and the meat should be opaque. (If you have a meat thermometer, the internal temperature should read at least 165 °F.) Cut chicken into ½-inch slices.

In a large bowl, toss lettuce, edamame, red onions, bell peppers, celery and chicken with the soy-ginger dressing, then divide among 4 plates. Sprinkle with almonds.

All in the Family

BY THE EARLY 1960s, we had opened 10 locations and business was booming. The original White Spot at 67th and Granville, in the big white-and-green log cabin, was in full swing, with the drive-in and dining room frequently packed. The White Spot at Lougheed Highway and Gilmore in Burnaby opened in 1961, and it became one of our most popular drive-ins, with carloads of kids dropping in on their way to the Pacific National Exhibition. That same year, we'd even gone outside the Lower Mainland, having opened our "overseas White Spot" at the Town and Country Shopping Centre in Saanich, on Vancouver Island. White Spot was still very much the place to go with friends, with a first date or with the folks for Sunday dinner.

There had been setbacks, as there always are. Nat's investment in a $250,000 White Spot dining room at the splashy new Oakridge

FACING: The drive-in at Georgia and Cardero in Vancouver. Pirate Paks were introduced on July 23, 1968.

Our Biggest Fan

ERWIN JELLEN stayed with us for 40 years, working his way up to manager. By the mid '60s, he was assistant manager at our Georgia and Cardero location, which still exists. He vividly remembers that the biggest drive-in order was from an American wrestler who was regularly in Vancouver for matches. His name was Haystacks Calhoun, and he weighed 600 pounds. He drove a big four-wheeler, and he'd pull into our drive-in and order five burgers. Then he'd order another five burgers. And another five. Each order of five burgers took the grill man less than five minutes to turn around, but it raised eyebrows in the kitchen.

"No kidding, he would order up to 45 hamburgers," says Erwin, laughing. "I'll never forget him."

Shopping Centre in Vancouver in 1959 had turned out to be a disappointment due to cost overruns. The Oakridge Room, despite rave reviews, never saw the popularity of the original White Spot Dining Room. But Nat had realized his entrepreneurial dream, and then some.

To keep menu items fresh as could be, Nat and his partners had centralized their baking and cooking operations with a major new 27,000-square-foot commissary at their Southeast Marine Drive location. They invested $1.5 million, which was a major expenditure at the time. Back then, if you'd walked into the commissary, you'd have found sides of beef hanging in the huge commercial refrigerators and turkeys roasting in the big ovens. The fresh-baked buns, pastries, cakes, pies, turkeys, chickens, hamburger patties, sauces and barbecued meats were prepared at the commissary and then delivered every morning to White Spot locations around Vancouver.

"The pie was so fresh and oozing with fruit that it was almost difficult to slice," recalls Al Hewlett, who, like Joe Scianna and Edwin Jellen, has been with White Spot since he was a kid. Al is a second-generation White Spot employee, which is not uncommon for our company. His father, Al Sr., was with White Spot from 1948 to 1986. "I like to say that, except for the first 20 years, there's always been an Al Hewlett working at White Spot," he says, laughing. Many families have been employed by White Spot: husbands and wives, parents and children, and now grandchildren.

Al started in 1969, and he met his wife, Kimberley, who is a hostess, on the job. Kim has been with White Spot for more than 30 years. They both work at the Broadway and Larch location in Vancouver, where they have long-time regulars who know them so well that Al and Kim are like an extended family. Kim must know about 1,000 of our guests by name, and that's not an exaggeration.

Today Al arrives for his shift at the very same White Spot he'd visit when he was five or six years old. He was there mornings, when the waitresses were making donuts and the air was filled with the vanilla and cinnamon aroma of the fresh cakes. You could buy a single donut for 10 cents or a pair for 15 cents. A coffee and a donut was a quarter. "If I hung around long enough, they'd give me a donut," says Al, laughing. "Everybody knew me."

And he got to know Nat because Al loves baseball. Nat taught Al Jr. how to keep score and gave him his first job, as scorekeeper. When Al was 16 and old enough to work at White Spot, he applied as a carhop at the Marine Drive location, which was close to his Richmond home. He didn't let his dad know in advance because he

Our first "overseas" White Spot opened at the Town and Country Shopping Centre in Saanich, B.C., in 1961.

wanted to be his own man and not rely on his father's help. Later he remembers being taught to serve the hugely popular, ultra-flaky, freshly made butterhorns that came in three flavours: cinnamon, lemon and walnut. When a guest ordered a butterhorn, Al wrapped it in parchment paper and toasted it on a small grill: "The parchment kept it from burning and the icing from melting." It was served hot, with a pat of cold butter on top. By the time it was served, on a white plate, to the guest, the butter was oozing perfectly over the sides of the golden pastry.

These days, Al works the breakfast shift, Monday through Friday. The White Spot Sunny Start breakfast, which is a mainstay, was born from serendipity in the 1960s. The kitchen staff would start their 8:30 a.m. shifts, and they'd cook up an egg sandwich for themselves. Back then, the restaurant didn't open until 10 a.m., so early breakfast items weren't a part of our menu.

When we started to open for breakfast at 6 a.m., it was a natural to include our staff's favourite breakfast sandwich, and today we call it the BC Sunny Start. The menu version, however, includes crispy bacon, Canadian cheddar, grilled vine-ripened tomato, a fried egg, our signature Triple "O" sauce, a soft bun and a side of hashbrowns. "I think part and parcel, Mr. Bailey believed you give a quality product, even down to the coffee. We've had our own brand and blend of coffee since I started," says Al.

Back in the day, you'd take a seat at our diner counter for a coffee and a slice of one of our pies, with soft ice cream. Our regulars loved the soft ice cream. But you might also have gone for a serving of Mrs. Bailey's popular plum pudding, or Al's mom Sunni's smooth-and-light refrigerator cheesecake, which Al Jr. remembers in detail to this day. She started with a flaky crust, which was spread with a thin layer of strawberry jam and topped with the cheesecake mixture and then garnished with whipped cream and nuts.

Making butter-horns at the White Spot Commissary, c. 1960-70s.

The White Spot
Junior Pipe Band in
front of city hall in
Vancouver, c. 1967.

Nat had the community on his mind as much as the food. He remained a devoted baseball fan and did whatever he could to promote the Mounties, a minor-league baseball club that launched in 1956, after the Oakland Oaks franchise relocated. He also made numerous contributions to charities near and dear to his heart. Today, we continue Nat's tradition of philanthropy with our commitment to sponsoring the White Spot Pipe Band, which had formed in 1956 but nearly ended until it found a major sponsor in Nat and White Spot, in 1963. The restaurant has sponsored the young band members ever since, as they journey around the world to events like the Calgary Stampede and the Beijing International Tourism Festival. We also support the Variety Show of Hearts Telethon, the Zajac Ranch for Children, CKNW Orphans' Fund, KidSport and various other children's charities. Community support and responsibility are a major part of the Nat Bailey legacy, and we gladly do our part.

By the end of the decade, Nat was a greatly admired, long-time high-profile B.C. businessman. He had recognized a demand for

Vancouver Mounties Baseball Club, 1960

Back Row: Dick Bielous, Trainer; Pat Gillick, P.; Dave Vineyard, P.; Walter Bond, O.F.; Howie Goss, O.F.; Fred Bacjewski, P.; Chet Nichols, P.; Joe Durham, O.F.; George Staller, Manager.
Middle Row: Bob Belinsky, P.; Charlie White, C.; Len Neal, C.; Jim Finigan, 3B.; Ray Barker, 1B.; Tony Alomar, 2B.; George Bamberger, coach; Jim Dyck, U.
Front Row: Wayne Causey, S.S.; Ron Moeller, P.; Neil Wilson, C.; Dave Jolly, P.; Chuck Oertel, O.F.; Phil Paine, P.; Julio Navarro, P.
Inset: Bobby Balcena, O.F.; Nat Bailey, President; Bob Freitas, General Manager; Joe Hatten, P.

PHOTO BY BOB McMANUS — KITSILANO DRUG

The 1960s Vancouver Mounties team.

quality, casual dining for a low price. He'd helped pioneer the concept, and he had built a thriving 13-restaurant drive-in and dining room operation that owned six Kentucky Fried Chicken franchises (all called Ernie's Fine Foods) and numerous other assets, including B.C.'s biggest chicken farm.

At 66 years old Nat was at retirement age, and on April 1, 1968, after 40 years in the restaurant business, he sold the White Spot chain to the giant American company, General Foods, for $6.5 million. He kept on as President of the White Spot Group. However, not entirely comfortable with the modern way of doing business, he quit a few months later to form a hotel management company, Bailey Hotels. His first purchase was the Villa Motor Hotel in Burnaby for $1.155 million cash, and he continued that business until his death in 1978. It was the end of an era, and the start of a whole new one.

Pirate Pak Is Born

JOE SCIANNA, his brother Andy and manager Brian Cunningham had been toying with the idea of creating a menu item just for kids, recalls Al Hewlett. "It was something that Brian and Andy and Joe thought about a lot and talked about a lot, what they could do for children," says Al.

Of course, we now know that the result of their brainstorming was the Pirate Pak, the whimsical cardboard ship with entrées like our Legendary Burgers, Chicken Pick'ns or grilled cheese sandwiches, accompanied by an ice cream and soft drink, drinking straw mast and chocolate doubloons.

Joe says, "The kids were asking for hamburgers, and they were too big. So we thought, 'Let's make a small burger and a little bun. You put the plate inside, add a Coke, a straw, some gold coins.' Nat Bailey loved it."

It was an instant hit, although the proto-type didn't look anything like the version we have today. "I think it looked like a shoe box," recalls Frank Leone, one of our long-time managers, laughing. "White Spot developed it further…and further."

One of the first restaurant meals designed exclusively for children, the Pirate Pak ushered in the era of family-casual dining—another first for White Spot. It is such a slice of B.C. child-hood history that we have even started an annual Pirate Pak day for adults, a fundraising event in support of Zajac Ranch for Children, an established B.C.-based charity that provides kids and young adults with serious medical conditions and chronic disabilities the chance to have an unforgettable summer camp experience. On Pirate Pak day, guests come into our restaurants dressed as pirates, their own kids in tow, celebrating their childhood nostalgia.

"I have so many people come in and talk to me and say how much they remember the Pirate Pak as kids," says Al. "That memory stuck with them for years and years and years. I served third-generation guests, and now I am starting to work on the fourth generation."

Legendary Burgers

Chuck Currie's
Favourite Burger

SERVES 4

1½ lbs lean ground beef (not extra-lean), formed in 4 patties

½ tsp kosher salt

½ tsp coarse black pepper

4 oz Cambozola cheese, in ¼-inch slices

1 Tbsp butter

1 large portobello mushroom, stem removed, and cap halved and cut in ¼-inch slices

4 good-quality, firm ciabatta or kaiser buns

¼ cup mayonnaise

2 Tbsp hamburger relish

4 leaf-lettuce leaves

2 vine-ripened tomatoes, in ¼-inch slices

OUR EXECUTIVE CHEF, Chuck Currie, has loved mushrooms ever since he discovered a hillside full of extremely rare morels on a neighbouring farm when he was a kid. The combination of meaty portobello mushrooms with Cambozola cheese on this burger is absolutely heavenly. Cambozola is a blend of Camembert and blue cheese, and even those who think they don't like blue cheese enjoy this dish. To serve this burger the White Spot way, top with a slice of dill pickle.

PREHEAT your barbecue to medium-high. Season burger patties on both sides with ¼ tsp of the salt and ¼ tsp of the pepper, then place them on the barbecue. Cook on 1 side for 5 minutes for a medium-well done burger, then flip the burger, and cook for 5 minutes more. (If you have a meat thermometer, the burgers should have an internal temperature of at least 165 °F when cooked.) Top each burger with slices of cheese.

In a small frying pan, melt butter on medium-high heat. Add mushrooms, season with the remaining ¼ tsp salt and ¼ tsp pepper and sauté until golden, about 1½ minutes per side.

While the mushrooms are cooking, toast the buns on the barbecue (or in a toaster oven). Spread the bottom half of each bun with mayonnaise and the hamburger relish. Top with lettuce and 2 slices of tomato and add the burgers. Spread the top half of the bun with the remaining mayonnaise. Divide mushrooms over the burgers and close the bun.

Bruschetta Burger

SERVES 4

1½ lbs lean ground beef (not extra-lean), formed in 4 patties

1 tsp kosher salt

1 tsp coarse black pepper

4 slices provolone cheese

4 good-quality, firm ciabatta or kaiser buns

¼ cup mayonnaise

4 leaf-lettuce leaves

¾ cup (¼ recipe) Bruschetta, drained (page 35)

BRUSCHETTA, IN ITALY, is not the tomato salsa we are showing you here—it is the bread you serve it on! It consists of grilled bread rubbed with garlic and topped with olive oil, salt and pepper. But we live in Canada, where bruschetta means a nice, fresh Italian tomato salsa. Here is our version, served in a delicious burger.

PREHEAT your barbecue to medium-high. Season burger patties on both sides with salt and pepper, then place them on the barbecue. Cook on 1 side for 5 minutes for a medium-well done burger, then flip the burger and cook for 4 minutes more. Top each burger with a slice of cheese and cook for another minute. (If you have a meat thermometer, the burgers should have an internal temperature of at least 165 °F when cooked.)

While the burgers are cooking, toast the buns on the barbecue (or in a toaster oven). Spread the bottom half of the bun with mayonnaise, then top with lettuce and a couple of tablespoons of bruschetta. Add the burger patties, close the bun and eat this baby over a plate with a few napkins at hand. Juicy!

Bacon Cheddar Burger

OUR VERY FIRST in the line of Bigger Burgers, this recipe combines two of the most popular burger toppings of all time: classic Canadian cheddar cheese and naturally hickory-smoked bacon.

PREHEAT your barbecue to medium-high. Season burger patties on both sides with salt and pepper, then place them on the barbecue. Cook on 1 side for 5 minutes for a medium-well-done burger, then flip the burger, and cook for 5 minutes more. (If you have a meat thermometer, the burgers should have an internal temperature of at least 165°F when cooked.) Top each burger with a slice of cheese.

Line a plate with paper towels. In a small frying pan, pan-fry bacon on medium heat until crispy, about 6 minutes. Drain bacon on the paper towel–lined plate.

While the bacon is cooking, toast the buns on the barbecue (or in a toaster oven). Spread the bottom half of each bun with mayonnaise, then top with lettuce, 2 slices of tomato and hamburger relish. Add the patties and 2 slices of bacon per serving. Spread the top half of the bun with the remaining mayonnaise and close over the burgers. Top with a slice of dill pickle.

SERVES 4

1½ lbs lean ground beef (not extra-lean), formed in 4 patties

½ tsp kosher salt

½ tsp coarse black pepper

4 slices medium cheddar cheese

8 slices thick-cut bacon

4 good-quality, firm ciabatta or kaiser buns

¼ cup mayonnaise

4 leaf-lettuce leaves

2 vine-ripened tomatoes, in ¼-inch slices

2 Tbsp hamburger relish

1 large dill pickle, chilled and sliced lengthwise

Caramelized Dijon Onion Burger

SWEET CARAMELIZED ONIONS and grainy Dijon mustard are a natural with burgers, especially when combined with a nutty cheese like fontina. Native to northern Italy, specifically to the Aosta Valley in the Alps, fontina has been produced since the twelfth century and tastes like a combination of Swiss cheese and mozzarella.

CARAMELIZED DIJON ONIONS Heat canola oil in a medium frying pan on medium. Add onions, pepper and mustard and cook, stirring frequently, until onions turn dark golden brown with a syrupy texture, about 20 minutes. Deglaze the bottom of the pan with vinegar. Remove from the heat and add Tabasco sauce and honey.

DIJON BURGERS Preheat your barbecue to medium-high. Season burger patties on both sides with salt and pepper, then place them on the barbecue. Cook on 1 side for 5 minutes for a medium-well-done burger, then flip the burger and cook for 5 minutes more. (If you have a meat thermometer, the burgers should have an internal temperature of at least 165 ° F when cooked.) Top each burger patty with a slice of cheese. Heat back bacon on the barbecue for 5 to 10 seconds per side, being sure not to dry it out.

While the burgers are cooking, toast the buns on the barbecue (or in a toaster oven). Spread the bottom half of the bun with mayonnaise and top with lettuce, 2 slices of tomato and some of the caramelized Dijon onions. Spread more caramelized onions on the top half of the bun, add the burger patties and a slice of back bacon, and close the bun.

SERVES 4

CARAMELIZED DIJON ONIONS

1½ tsp canola oil

1 onion, in ⅛-inch slices (1½ cups)

1 tsp coarse black pepper

½ cup grainy Dijon mustard

1 Tbsp malt vinegar

¼ tsp Tabasco sauce

¼ cup liquid honey

DIJON BURGERS

1½ lbs lean ground beef (not extra-lean), formed in 4 patties

½ tsp kosher salt

½ tsp coarse black pepper

4 slices fontina cheese

4 slices back bacon

4 good-quality, firm ciabatta or kaiser buns

2 Tbsp mayonnaise

4 leaf-lettuce leaves

2 vine-ripened tomatoes, in ¼-inch slices

Peanut Butter, Bacon & Jalapeño Burger

SERVES 4

1½ lbs lean ground beef (not extra-lean), formed in 4 patties

½ tsp kosher salt

½ tsp coarse black pepper

4 good-quality, firm ciabatta or kaiser buns

2 Tbsp mayonnaise

4 leaf-lettuce leaves

2 vine-ripened tomatoes, in ¼-inch slices

½ cup crunchy peanut butter

8 slices thick-cut bacon, cooked crisp and crumbled

32 slices canned jalapeño peppers, drained

THIS BURGER WAS first developed by our Executive Development Chef, Danny Markowicz, for our popular Burger Guest Stars promotion because we wanted to do something a little unexpected for our more daring guests. It may sound crazy, but our taste testers discovered this unlikely combination of sweet, crunchy peanut butter; crisp, smokey bacon; and slightly spicy jalapeño peppers was the perfect marriage.

For a special treat, spread jalapeño jelly over the peanut butter before you add the bacon bits. The combination of spicy, sweet, savoury and smokey is like a party in your mouth.

PREHEAT your barbecue to medium-high. Season burger patties on both sides with salt and pepper, then place them on the barbecue. Cook on 1 side for 5 minutes for a medium-well done burger, then flip the burger and cook for 5 minutes more. (If you have a meat thermometer, the burgers should have an internal temperature of at least 165°F when cooked.)

While the burgers are cooking, toast the buns on the barbecue (or in a toaster oven). Spread the bottom half of the bun with mayonnaise and top with lettuce and 2 slices of tomato. Spread the top half of the bun with peanut butter and sprinkle with bacon bits and jalapeño slices. Add the burger patties and close the bun.

Thai Chicken Burger

BEFORE YOU MAKE this burger, you may need to make a trip to your local Asian market for a few ingredients for the gai yang marinade and peanut sauce. Gai yang means "barbecued (or grilled) chicken" and is a common street food in Thailand. Thai red curry paste is available in many stores; we prefer the Mae Ploy brand because of its balance of dried red chilies, garlic, shallots, lemon grass, galangal, shrimp paste and kaffir lime peel, but any red curry paste will work. Look for sambal oelek, a puréed Indonesian hot pepper sauce, and ketjap manis, a sweet Indonesian soy sauce, at specialty food shops.

GAI YANG-MARINATED CHICKEN Place garlic, ginger, cilantro, red curry paste, sugar, soy sauce and turmeric in a food processor and purée until smooth.

Place chicken breasts in a large bowl or a resealable plastic bag, pour the marinade overtop and ensure chicken is completely covered. Refrigerate from 1 to 3 hours (the longer, the more intense the flavour).

PEANUT SAUCE Combine all ingredients in a food processor and purée until smooth.

THAI CHICKEN BURGERS Preheat the barbecue to medium. Place marinated chicken breasts on the grill and rotate them after a minute so that they don't stick and so that they become marked with nice crossed grill marks. Flip the chicken after 4 minutes, and cook for another 4 minutes, rotating the meat on the grill. To test for doneness, poke along the grain with your tongs at the thickest point. The juices should run clear and the meat should be opaque. (If you have a meat thermometer, the internal temperature should read 165°F.)

While the chicken is cooking, toast the buns on the barbecue (or in a toaster oven). Spread mayonnaise on the top half of the bun and cover with 2 slices of tomato and red onions. Spread peanut sauce on the bottom half of the bun and top with cucumber slices and bean sprouts. Add chicken, close the bun and Thai on your eating apron!

SERVES 4

GAI YANG-
MARINATED CHICKEN

¼ cup minced garlic

2 Tbsp finely grated
fresh ginger

1 bunch fresh cilantro

1 Tbsp Thai red curry paste

2 tsp granulated sugar

½ cup low-sodium soy sauce

3 Tbsp turmeric

4 skinless, boneless
chicken breasts, each 4 oz

PEANUT SAUCE

2 Tbsp smooth peanut butter

2 tsp water

1½ tsp rice vinegar

½ tsp sambal oelek

2 tsp ketjap manis

¼ tsp minced garlic

¼ tsp finely
grated fresh ginger

1 Tbsp chopped
fresh cilantro

THAI CHICKEN BURGERS

4 Gai Yang-Marinated
Chicken breasts

4 good-quality, firm
ciabatta or kaiser buns

¼ cup mayonnaise

2 vine-ripened tomatoes,
in ¼-inch slices

4 very thin slices red onion

16 slices English cucumber

Large handful of
fresh bean sprouts

Mediterranean Chicken Burger

SERVES 4

CREAM CHEESE SPREAD

¼ cup spreadable cream cheese

2 Tbsp sour cream

1½ tsp fresh lemon juice

2 tsp diced red onions

2 Tbsp unpeeled, diced English cucumber

1 tsp capers, drained

LEMON GRILLING SAUCE

1 Tbsp extra-virgin olive oil

4 tsp minced garlic

Pinch of dried whole-leaf rosemary

2 pinches dried whole-leaf oregano

1½ tsp kosher salt

¾ tsp coarse black pepper

2 Tbsp fresh lemon juice

CHICKEN BURGERS

4 skinless, boneless chicken breasts, each 4 oz

4 good-quality, firm ciabatta or kaiser buns

4 leaf-lettuce leaves

2 vine-ripened tomatoes, in ¼-inch slices

1 red bell pepper, seeded and sliced in ¼-inch rings

12 slices English cucumber

¼ cup crumbled goat's milk feta cheese

THIS BURGER WAS inspired by Bearfoot Bistro's Executive Chef, Melissa Craig, who loves Greek salad and Greek food in general. The lemon grilling sauce for the chicken is a perfect match for the refreshing cream cheese spread and also complements our Santorini Chicken Salad.

CREAM CHEESE SPREAD Combine all ingredients until well mixed. Set aside.

LEMON GRILLING SAUCE Combine ingredients in a small jar until well mixed.

CHICKEN BURGERS Preheat the barbecue to medium. Brush chicken breasts with lemon grilling sauce and place them on the grill. Rotate chicken breasts after a minute so that they don't stick and so that they become marked with nice crossed grill marks. Flip the chicken after 4 minutes, and cook for another 4 minutes, rotating the meat on the grill. To test for doneness, poke along the grain with your tongs at the thickest point. The juices should run clear and the meat should be opaque. (If you have a meat thermometer, the internal temperature should read at least 165 °F.)

While chicken is cooking, toast the buns on the barbecue (or in a toaster oven). Spread both halves of the bun with about 1 Tbsp of the cream cheese spread. Top with lettuce, 2 slices tomatoes, bell pepper rings, cucumber slices and feta. Add chicken, close the bun and dig in.

Wild Pacific Salmon Burger

WILD PACIFIC SOCKEYE, coho or red spring salmon are all great options for this burger.

LEMON-BASIL AIOLI Whisk together ingredients and refrigerate for at least 1 hour to allow the flavours to blend.

LEMON-BASIL-TARRAGON BUTTER Combine ingredients until well mixed and set aside.

SALMON BURGERS Season salmon fillets with salt and pepper. Heat lemon-basil-tarragon butter in a nonstick pan on medium heat and pan-fry fillets for 4 minutes per side. Using a fork, pull apart the thickest part of the fillet along the fish's natural seams. When ⅛ inch at the very centre is still a little dark pink and not milky, remove salmon from the heat. (The fish will cook through to just done as you are dressing the buns.)

While the salmon is cooking, toast the buns. Spread both cut sides with lemon-basil aioli. Top the bottom half of each bun with a lettuce leaf and 2 tomato slices. Place a salmon fillet over the tomatoes, close the bun and brag to your friends that White Spot taught you to make this!

SERVES 4

LEMON-BASIL AIOLI

½ cup mayonnaise

¼ cup finely chopped fresh basil leaves

1 tsp minced garlic

1½ Tbsp fresh lemon juice

LEMON-BASIL-TARRAGON BUTTER

¼ cup melted butter, cooled a little so that it doesn't "cook" the herbs

2 Tbsp fresh lemon juice

1 tsp chopped fresh tarragon

1½ tsp chopped fresh basil leaves

1 tsp chopped fresh parsley

SALMON BURGERS

4 skinless, boneless wild salmon fillets, each 4 oz

¼ tsp kosher salt

¼ tsp coarse black pepper

4 good-quality, firm ciabatta or kaiser buns

4 leaf-lettuce leaves

2 vine-ripened tomatoes, in ¼-inch slices, sprinkled with kosher salt and black pepper

Transition Time

T HE 1970S HAD arrived, and young people had moved on to hard rock and disco, playing that funky music, doing the hustle, wearing toe socks and tuxedo T-shirts, and making Doodle Art. Having survived the political upheaval of the late 1960s, the youth were less naive than their parents' generation, and more aware. The era was also positively outlandish, however, with crazy wide-flare pants, Elton John–style sunglasses, rainbow Afros, Pet Rocks, mood rings and the "streaking" craze.

Instant food was all the rage, even though Julia Child was cooking up a storm on TV and Irma Rombauer's 1975 *Joy of Cooking* edition had come along. Entertaining usually involved spinach dip, Swedish meatballs, a cheese fondue and, of course, cocktails. At White Spot, we kept it homestyle and simple, with comfort-food dinners like

FACING: Vancouver's youth have always flocked to White Spot for good food, good times and good friends.

roast turkey and mashed potatoes, pasta dishes, clubhouse sand-
wiches, and regular items like our famous award-winning burgers.
Our drive-ins were still going strong, and our dining room on Gran-
ville Street was still the place to go for birthdays and anniversaries.
"Sunday night dinners at Granville were huge by the time I worked at
White Spot in the '70s," says long-time employee Al Hewlett.

Pat Quinn was a talented young hockey player from Ontario who
was snapped up by the Vancouver Canucks during the NHL Expansion Draft in 1970. White Spot celebrated the Canucks' expansion
by offering gift certificates to the team member awarded Player of
the Game. "I had won one night, and I got to use the certificate at
White Spot," recalls Pat. "My kids enjoyed going there, so it became
a regular place for us to visit. With two young kids, that was our
night out. Other players would win it as well, so the whole team
eventually went there. We were from out of town, and we were all
introduced to White Spot, and we all became fans."

General Foods, based in White Plains, New York, with a Canadian office in Toronto, had big plans for their new restaurant
venture. They immediately built five new Kentucky Fried Chicken
locations and two new White Spot drive-ins, and they enlarged the
White Spot at Broadway and Larch, and the White Spot commissary, which was renamed Quality Kitchens. The logo got an update,
as did the restaurants, which were redesigned with the booths and
valance lighting that were popular at the time. It was in the 1970s
when White Spot transitioned from coffee shop to full-on, licenced
restaurant, with a more extensive menu and more sophisticated
food-service operation.

"General Foods brought White Spot into the more modern time,"
says Peter Toigo Jr. "They expanded the concept."

General Foods also changed the culture at White Spot, which
made the 1970s a period of adjustment. Employees used to Nat's
solid, old-style, hands-on approach were suddenly dealing with a
distant corporate culture. "It's not the same as being run by an individual family or entrepreneur, where you are hands on," says Peter.
"You're running it from a boardroom somewhere else and changing
presidents every year almost. So you don't have that continuity."

Spot Staffers Show Heart

W E BECAME a supporter of Variety, the Children's Charity, in the mid 1960s and have been a major supporter of Show of Hearts Telethon since its inception. To this day, about 140 of our employees and our suppliers donate their time each year to help feed the Variety volunteers involved in the 24-hour telethon. Today, the typical grocery list for the job includes 3,500 hamburgers, 800 litres of soup, 1,200 sandwiches, hundreds of desserts and lots more. Without hesitation, our staff work tirelessly—we even have an overnight shift—to keep the telethon volunteers fed throughout the long night. We are also a supporter of Variety's Got Talent, an event that supports young, talented performers in our province. In 2011, Peter Sr. was honoured with the Gold Heart Award, and in 2012, White Spot was recognized with the Variety International Corporate Award, an honour bestowed upon only nine companies worldwide.

Peter Toigo Sr.

B.C.'s famous rock 'n' roll disc jockey Red Robinson remembers a few changes that didn't go over too well with his mother, who'd been a White Spot manager since 1950, when Red was 12 years old. "She loved working for Nat," says Red. He remembers that under the new owners a beloved drink called Honey Dew came off the menu, replaced by Tang, the super-sweet orange drink made famous by an advertising campaign that said it was a favourite with astronauts. Honey Dew was a Vancouver institution, and there was even a Honey Dew chain of restaurants throughout the city at one time. "My mother said, 'They are wrecking my White Spot with this crummy Tang,'" recalls Red, laughing.

At the start of the 1980s, we had combined sales of about $100 million. But General Foods' restaurants south of the border weren't faring nearly so well, and the company opted to sell off its White Spot division. Enter Peter C. Toigo, an entrepreneur and developer born in Powell River, B.C., who was a long-time fan of Nat's. "He admired guys like H.R. MacMillan and Nat Bailey, and all those self-made entrepreneurs that have that innovative way," says Peter Jr., who, along with Ron, took over as Managing Director of Shato Holdings when Peter Sr. died in 1993.

In 1982, the company accepted an offer from Peter Sr., who, like Nat, had a big-picture vision and an innovative entrepreneurial spirit that began when he was a young kid who knew the art of the hustle. And we don't mean the dance. Like Nat, who sold peanuts roadside out of his Model T, Peter had begun finessing the art of the business deal as a kid, selling grapes to winemakers and collecting empty beer bottles. By 17, he and his parents had bought the Wildwood Grocery Store in a suburb of Powell River, and, by 18, he was married to his high school sweetheart, Elizabeth Rohver. That same year, he purchased a dairy with a small down payment. The dairy helped him launch a career as a property developer, ultimately leading to the development of shopping centres, hotels and residential properties.

After extensive negotiation, Peter Sr. owned his dream business, White Spot Limited. As well, he found himself the owner of properties he didn't even know were included in the deal, such as 54 KFC restaurants, ICL Catering contracts and an Ontario-based company called Crock & Block restaurants. His assertive style didn't stop at his new venture. When he took over, he appointed former General Foods executive Peter T. Main as President and CEO of the company and embarked on the biggest expansion plan in White Spot's history. We opened new restaurants in Kelowna, Abbotsford and Nanaimo.

"Peter Toigo had a passion for B.C. He was the White Spot diner that we all were, and he revived it in the minds of people," says Red Robinson. "The first thing he did was get rid of Tang," he adds, laughing.

A few years after the change in ownership, in February 1986, the beloved White Spot at 67th and Granville Street burned down. It had just recently been renovated, but flames made short order of the shingle roof and dry timber frame. Teary-eyed crowds gathered to watch the heritage building burn beyond repair.

The old White Spot might have been lost, but on the bright side, Peter Sr. had his sights on major expansion into new markets and a more up-to-date White Spot. Peter Sr. understood that there was a new segment of the market—people who wanted healthy options when they ate out. "If a group of people go out for dinner, you want to be sure there are menu items for everyone in that group," says Warren Erhart, our long-time President who started with

Carhop at our Georgia and Cardero drive-in with members of the White Spot Pipe Band, c. 1970s.

us during the Peter Sr. years. "If one person wants a big salad and it's not on the menu, the entire group will go elsewhere. That's a problem."

And so, after meeting the Executive Chef at California's Pritikin Longevity Centre, Peter decided to develop a menu that would meet established nutritional standards. Pritikin's chef, Nicolas Klontz, came to Vancouver to act as a consultant for the program, and the menu soon featured low-fat, low-sodium dishes. Peter Sr. was way ahead of his time. (Later, in 2007, White Spot became the first B.C. restaurant chain to embrace the Health Check Program, a Heart and Stroke Foundation healthy lifestyle initiative.)

Nat may have been a burgers and fried chicken guy, but he would likely have approved of the Toigo approach to constantly keeping up with the times. "It's a bit of a challenge because as you keep evolving in what you do, you can't throw the baby out with the bathwater," Warren says. "You have to stay relevant in everything that you do,

The fire that burned the original White Spot Dining Room on Granville at 67th in Vancouver was front-page news.

VANCOUVER, B.C. **The Sun** SATURDAY, FEBRUARY 8, 1986 75 cents minimum outside Lower Mainland

City urged to ban smoking in public buildings

By KARENN KRANGLE
Sun City Hall Bureau

Vancouver's health department is recommending new amendments to the health bylaw that will make it illegal to smoke in most non-residential buildings in the city.

Smoking would be outlawed in:
Cinemas, theatres and libraries.
Retail shops, bank service lines and counters.
Hospitals, clinics, medical and dental offices.
All public and government buildings.
Pools and other indoor sporting facilities.
Schools and display areas in museums and galleries.
Those not enforcing the laws or smokers who disobey

them could risk fines of $50 to $2,000, plus $50 a day for continuing offences.

While the proposed amendments allow for employers, businesses, restaurants and others to provide special smoking areas, health officers want city hall to make it clear that smokers are the exception to the norm.

And they have recommended that employers who cannot solve disputes between employees over smoking on the job simply prohibit the use of tobacco.

"All persons in Vancouver have the right to breathe clean indoor air in places of public assembly and in the workplace, and no individual has the right to pollute the air of others with substances known to be hazardous to health," said a report to council detailing the bylaw changes.

It noted that it will be more difficult to regulate the no-smoking laws in the workplace than in other areas, but the proposed amendments are meant to "offer employees basic minimum rights to clean indoor air."

John Dixon, president of the B.C. Civil Liberties Association, said he doesn't foresee private businesses taking legal action if the bylaw is passed by council.

"I suspect that the health department probably does have the authority to restrict the noxious presence of matters such as smoke," he said Friday.

Dixon compared smoking in private buildings to spreading a communicable disease.

"I doubt that the city health department would find its jurisdiction only in public places in this case," he said.

"The health department is saying that second-hand

smoke poses a substantial threat to the health of employees who have no wish to be exposed to it."

Dixon said the association has not yet had time to study the proposed bylaw with a view to taking a position on it.

Currently, the bylaw only restricts smoking where food is prepared or displayed. The fire bylaw prohibits smoking in large stores and other areas considered a fire hazard.

The report said about 74 per cent of Vancouver adults do not smoke, and surveys that independent random surveys have indicated that more than 90 per cent of the population favors smoking restrictions in public places that about 21 per cent wanted no smoking in restaurants.

"Smoking," A2

Marcos hints he'll scrap vote

Sun News Dispatches

MANILA — President Ferdinand Marcos raised the possibility today that he might declare the just-held presidential election invalid and serve out the remainder of his term.

"As of now, I am just trying to play it by ear," Marcos said in response to a news conference question as to what he would do if U.S. election observers found Friday's voting had been "unclean."

There have been continuing charges of irregularities amid widespread reports of voter intimidation, vote-buying and ballot box switching in the election between Marcos and opposition candidate Corazon Aquino.

Earlier today, Aquino, a political novice who was showing a growing lead against Marcos in the government's own unofficial tally, called on the president to concede defeat.

The latest count from the Marcos-appointed Commission of Elections, or COME-LEC, showed the 53-year-old widow of assassinated opposition leader Benigno Aquino with a 51.20-per-cent lead.

In Washington, the U.S. state department said election results from a volunteer civic organization, the National Movement for Free Elections (NAMFREL), showed Aquino with 3.3 million votes to 2.5 million for Marcos.

Namfrel is endorsed by U.S. officials and the Roman Catholic Church.

Opponents have suggested that should Marcos, 68, find himself in danger of losing to Aquino, he might invoke his constitutional powers to halt the process and stay in office. Marcos, who has held power for 20 years, said that before considering the possibility of an election process, he would first try

Candidates' relatives walk; violent prospects, A15

INSIDE

☐ PROBE WANTED: Thomas Sophonow, tried three times for a Winnipeg murder before being finally acquitted and released, wants the conduct of his case probed. H9

COUNTDOWN **EXPO 86** 83 DAYS TO GO

☐ LOTTERY: A2

☐ WEATHER: It will be mainly sunny in the city on Sunday, with early morning fog patches. F1

☐ CRICKET BREAK: Rick in Australia on his Man in

RESTAURANT BURNS

— Peter Battistoni photo
FLAMES leap from roof of White Spot Restaurant at 67th and Granville as firemen fight fire that badly damaged building Friday. (Story, A3.)

Curfew set in Haiti after 10 di

Sun News Dispatches

PORT-AU-PRINCE — As Haiti's new military-civilian council imposed a curfew on outbursts of wild celebration mixed with looting, former president-for-life Jean-Claude Duvalier settled into the French Alpine resort of Talloires while France sought a country willing to offer him refuge.

The six-man "national council of government" headed by army chief of staff Lt.-Gen. Henri Namphy ordered a 2 p.m.-to-5 a.m. curfew after 10 members of the military reported slain in revenge killings.

Duvalier and 22 others, mainly members of his family, left Haiti Friday aboard a

Picture, A2; Editorial, A4

Force plane, ending 28 years of family rule in this impoverished Caribbean country where the average per capita annual income is U.S.

Duvalier, his wife Michele, two children and a 22-member entourage settled into an exclusive lakeside hotel near the border.

Residents said they understood he would remain in Talloires at least the weekend and possibly longer.

A foreign ministry spokesman said Friday that Duvalier would stay for "a few eight days at the most.

Guests who had been staying at the baye hotel were asked to move out to make room for Duvalier and his party.

Duvalier was granted permission to France was efforts were made by other country that would accept him, western diplomatic sources said.

Canada has received but not yet a direct request to grant political asylum to Duvalier, external affairs spokesman Brady said Friday.

Brady added that Ottawa realizes Canada would not welcome Duvalier.

"It it is true, as the Prime Minister

"Duvalier," A2

Red's Rock 'n' Roll Reunion

RED ROBINSON has interviewed Elvis and the Beatles and every rock 'n' roll star from back in the day. He's been a high-profile radio personality his whole life—and one of our biggest fans, visiting our drive-in regularly for a chocolate shake and a clubhouse. "White Spot is a part of my life, and it is for all of us who grew up in Vancouver. And that's not just a cliché," he says.

Red is a fan, but he's also been a part of the White Spot family. In 1982, Red, who co-owned an ad agency, worked with Peter C. Toigo on an advertising campaign, "Nothing else tastes like White Spot," to rekindle memories of what has made us a beloved institution. Just three years later his mom, Alice, earned our diamond service pin for 35 years of service when she retired from White Spot.

That same year, White Spot sponsored Red's rock 'n' roll reunion concert at the Pacific Coliseum, which included Chuck Berry, Bobby Curtola, the Chiffons and Freddy Cannon. On

the day of the show, several of the artists from the lineup performed at our Granville Street location, to the absolute delight of a big crowd. The concept worked so well that Red brought in 41 legends to perform at Expo 86, including Jerry Lee Lewis and Fats Domino. "Every Sunday we had a matinee, and it was a huge success," he recalls, and "White Spot made it possible because of the Coliseum show."

whether it's menu development, décor, training programs or our service. It's about staying current.

"I get calls from people that say Nat wouldn't approve of this or that, but the thing is, he was assertive and innovative. He would probably find ways. Now, more than ever, you have to be nimble. There are so many great competitors." To operate efficiently alongside higher real estate prices, a changing demographic, emerging markets and changing tastes, though, White Spot continues to do what it has always done best. In the 1990s, the Toigos helped us take Nat's concept of customer service and fresh food to a whole new level.

For Red Robinson's 50th birthday, artist Bruce Stewart drew this illustration of Red as a young DJ with his wife and local radio collegues at the original White Spot on Granville & 67th.

Pastas & Rice Bowls

Mushroom-Prosciutto Cannelloni *82*

Parmesan Chicken with Ravioli *85*

"What's-in-the-Sauce?"
Spaghetti Marinara & Meatballs *87*

Fettuccine Alfredo *89*

Salmon, Prawn & Scallop Risotto *90*

Prawn Risotto with Champagne Sauce *92*

Teriyaki Chicken Rice Bowl *93*

Salmon Shiitake Rice Bowl *95*

Prawn & Lentil Rice Bowl *96*

Sukiyaki Rice Bowl *98*

Mushroom-Prosciutto Cannelloni

SERVES 4 TO 6

SPICY TOMATO SAUCE

1¼ Tbsp extra-virgin olive oil

¼ onion, diced (about ¼ cup)

2½ tsp minced garlic

¾ tsp kosher salt

¼ tsp coarse black pepper

Pinch of crushed chilies

¼ tsp cayenne pepper

2 dashes Tabasco sauce

1 can (14 fl oz/398 mL) tomatoes, drained and chopped

Pinch of granulated sugar

1 cup whipping cream

½ cup white wine

1¼ Tbsp chopped fresh basil leaves

1¼ Tbsp grated Italian parmesan cheese

CANNELLONI

2 Tbsp extra-virgin olive oil

¼ onion, diced (about ¼ cup)

4 tsp minced garlic

¼ tsp coarse black pepper

1⅔ cups sliced crimini mushrooms

3 slices prosciutto, in ½-inch strips

1 cup ricotta cheese

¼ cup chopped fresh parsley

2 tsp grated lemon zest

10 sheets fresh pasta, each about 6 × 4 inches

½ cup grated Italian parmesan cheese

PERFECT TOMATO SAUCES start with perfect tomatoes! Don't use fresh tomatoes. Some vine-ripened tomatoes are wonderful for salads and sandwiches, but they're too juicy for tomato sauce. You want meaty tomatoes, like San Marzano or Roma or plum tomatoes, and the best ones are the canned Italian varieties. It's not necessary to simmer a nice tomato sauce very much at all—that's for meat sauces—as tomatoes lose flavour the more you cook them. Use good tomatoes and you will hardly have to add any other ingredients.

Homemade pasta sheets are the easiest to use; however, if you use store-bought sheets for this cannelloni, soak them in warm water for 30 to 60 seconds to make them pliable before filling. Serve with garlic bread and a nice green salad.

SPICY TOMATO SAUCE Heat olive oil in a saucepan on medium. Add onions, garlic, salt, pepper, chilies, cayenne and Tabasco sauce and cook until onions are just translucent, 5 to 6 minutes. Stir in tomatoes, sugar, cream and white wine and simmer, covered, for 10 minutes. Remove from the heat and stir in basil and parmesan. Will keep refrigerated for up to 5 days.

CANNELLONI Preheat the oven to 350 °F. Heat olive oil in a medium frying pan on medium. Add onions, garlic, pepper and mushrooms and cook until onions are translucent and mushrooms are nicely browned, 5 to 6 minutes.

In a food processor, combine ½ of the onion mixture with the prosciutto and process, pulsing about 10 times, until coarsely chopped. (Do not allow this mixture to purée.) Transfer this mixture to a bowl and stir in the remaining mushroom mixture, along with the ricotta, parsley and lemon zest.

Arrange pasta sheets on a clean work surface. Place ¼ cup filling in a line about 1 inch from the bottom edge of each pasta sheet. Fold the bottom edge of the pasta over the filling and roll snugly until you have a tube about 6 inches wide and 1½ inches thick. Repeat until you have 10 filled cannelloni.

Set out a large rectangular ovenproof baking dish, about
9 × 12 inches, large enough to hold all of the cannelloni in a
single layer. Ladle ⅓ of the spicy tomato sauce into the bottom of
the baking dish, spreading to cover the entire surface. Arrange
cannelloni over the sauce, ensuring the edges of the pasta don't
touch each other. Cover with the rest of the sauce, making sure
the pasta is well covered by sauce on all sides. Sprinkle with
parmesan and bake for about 30 minutes, or until sauce and
filling are steaming hot and pasta is cooked through. Garnish
with parsley and serve immediately, family style.

Parmesan Chicken

WITH RAVIOLI

WE HAVE SERVED this ravioli during our Winter Comfort Foods promotion, but in warmer weather you can substitute spinach-ricotta ravioli for the mushroom version. Either way, serve with garlic bread or focaccia and a sprig of oregano.

PREHEAT the oven to 450°F. In a small bowl, combine olive oil, parmesan, oregano and garlic until well mixed. Season chicken breasts with ¼ tsp of the salt and pepper and arrange them in a baking dish. Cover evenly with the parmesan mixture, patting it on to the top of each one. Bake for about 9 minutes until the chicken is just cooked and the cheese coating has melted and browned onto the chicken. To test for doneness, poke along the grain of the chicken at the thickest point. The juices should run clear and the meat should be opaque. (If you have a meat thermometer, the internal temperature should read at least 165°F.)

While the chicken is cooking, simmer ravioli in a large pot of boiling water with salt and canola oil for 7 to 10 minutes. (The oil floats on the water and prevents any foam from the pasta from boiling over.) The ravioli is ready when the pasta casing is soft and fully cooked. Drain the pasta.

In a large saucepan on medium heat, toss ravioli with marinara sauce until it is bubbling. Divide the pasta and sauce among 4 plates or bowls. Top each serving with parmesan chicken and sprinkle with parsley.

SERVES 4

2 Tbsp extra-virgin olive oil

1 cup grated Italian parmesan cheese

1 Tbsp chopped fresh oregano leaves

1 Tbsp minced garlic

4 skinless, boneless chicken breasts, each 4 oz

1 Tbsp + ¼ tsp kosher salt

¼ tsp coarse black pepper

16 to 24 large- to medium-size mushroom ravioli

2 Tbsp canola oil

3 cups (1 recipe) "What's-in-the-Sauce?" Marinara Sauce (page 88)

2 Tbsp chopped fresh parsley

Spaghetti Marinara & Meatballs

"WHAT'S IN THE sauce?" was Umberto Menghi's line while tasting this sauce in two of our "Fresh Thinking. Fresh Cooking" TV ads. A renowned Italian chef, he brought authentic Italian cooking to the West Coast when he opened Umberto's, his first restaurant in Vancouver, in 1973. Today he continues his legacy of world-class cooking and hospitality at his two restaurants in Whistler.

The meatballs are a fantastic addition to the basic spaghetti marinara, but they're optional. You can make them ahead of time, refrigerate them and warm them up in a microwave, but they are unbelievably delicious straight out of the oven! Cook the sauce and the spaghetti while the meatballs are baking.

Extra parmesan for sprinkling on top of this spaghetti is also a great addition. So is focaccia or garlic bread. Another real treat is to throw on at the end some exotic mushrooms sautéed with a little olive oil and/or butter, some salt and pepper, a little garlic and just a drop of truffle oil!

MEATBALLS Preheat the oven to 350°F. Line a baking sheet with parchment paper.

Heat olive oil in a small pan on medium. Add onions, garlic, salt, pepper and marjoram and cook until onions are just translucent, 5 to 6 minutes. Allow to cool to room temperature.

Place the onion mixture in a large bowl. Add ground meats, oats, milk, egg, parsley and parmesan and mix by hand until just combined nicely. Using your hands, form 12 meatballs, each about 2 inches in diameter. Arrange them on the baking sheet and roast for about 20 minutes. (If you have a meat thermometer, the internal temperature should read at least 165°F. The meatballs will no longer be pink in the middle.) *continued overleaf >*

SERVES 4

MEATBALLS

1 Tbsp extra-virgin olive oil

½ onion, in ¼-inch dice (¾ cup)

2 Tbsp minced garlic

1½ tsp kosher salt

1 tsp coarse black pepper

½ tsp dried whole-leaf marjoram

¾ lb medium ground beef

6 oz ground pork

¼ cup rolled oats

2 Tbsp milk

1 large egg

2 Tbsp chopped fresh parsley

¼ cup grated Italian parmesan cheese

MARINARA SAUCE

¼ cup extra-virgin olive oil

½ onion, in
¼-inch dice (¾ cup)

1½ tsp minced garlic

½ tsp dried
whole-leaf oregano

½ tsp dried
whole-leaf rosemary

½ tsp dried whole-leaf thyme

1½ tsp kosher salt

1½ tsp coarse black pepper

3 cans (each 14 fl oz/398 mL)
tomatoes, puréed

½ cup grated Italian
parmesan cheese

SPAGHETTI

12 oz dried Italian spaghetti

1 Tbsp kosher salt

2 Tbsp canola oil

½ cup finely chopped
fresh basil leaves

¼ cup chopped fresh parsley

MARINARA SAUCE Heat olive oil in a large saucepan on medium. Add onions, garlic, oregano, rosemary, thyme, salt and pepper and cook until onions are just translucent, 5 to 6 minutes. Add tomatoes, increase the heat to medium-high, cover and bring to a boil. Reduce the heat to low, add meatballs and stir in parmesan. Set aside.

SPAGHETTI Cook spaghetti in a large pot of boiling water with salt and canola oil for about 6 minutes. (The oil floats on the water and prevents any foam from the pasta from boiling over.) The pasta is ready when a faint "line" of uncooked pasta is still visible in the centre of a noodle when you cut across it. This tiny bit of uncooked pasta will cook out when you simmer it with the sauce. Your pasta will be "al dente" (literally "to the tooth" in Italian)—fully cooked but not soggy.

Drain the spaghetti well and immediately add it to the marinara sauce. Bring to a simmer on medium heat and then toss in basil. Divide among 4 plates or serve family style in 1 big bowl. Sprinkle with parsley and serve immediately.

Fettuccine Alfredo

STIRRING LONG NOODLES while they cook helps prevent them from clumping. Once you add them to the boiling water, wait a minute until the pasta softens, then stir almost constantly with a pair of long tongs until the noodles are cooked al dente. Drain the pasta in a colander, flush it quickly with just enough cold water to remove any excess starch, toss it with the sauce and allow it to finish cooking.

ALFREDO SAUCE Heat cream, butter, garlic, salt, pepper and nutmeg in a large saucepan on medium. Simmer until reduced to 3 cups, about 10 minutes. Reduce heat to low and stir in parmesan. Remove from the heat and set aside.

FETTUCCINE Cook fettuccine in a large pot of boiling water with salt and canola oil for about 7 minutes. (The oil floats on the water and prevents any foam from the pasta from boiling over.) The pasta is ready when a faint "line" of uncooked pasta is still visible in the centre of a noodle when you cut across it. This tiny bit of uncooked pasta will cook out when you simmer it with the sauce. Your pasta will be "al dente" (literally "to the tooth" in Italian)— fully cooked but not soggy.

TOMATO-BASIL SALSA While the pasta is cooking, toss tomatoes, basil, red onions, salt and pepper together in a bowl.

FINISH FETTUCCINE Drain the pasta and immediately transfer to a large saucepan and add the Alfredo sauce. Bring it to a simmer on medium-high heat. Divide among 4 plates or bowls, garnish with the tomato-basil salsa and parsley and serve immediately.

SERVES 4

ALFREDO SAUCE
4 cups whipping cream

½ lb unsalted butter (1 cup)

2 Tbsp minced garlic

1 tsp kosher salt

1 tsp coarse black pepper

½ tsp nutmeg

1 cup grated Italian parmesan cheese

FETTUCCINE
1 lb high-quality dried fettuccine, Italian preferred

1 Tbsp kosher salt

2 Tbsp canola oil

2 Tbsp chopped fresh parsley

TOMATO-BASIL SALSA
8 large cherry tomatoes, quartered

2 Tbsp finely chopped fresh basil leaves

2 Tbsp diced red onions

¼ tsp kosher salt

¼ tsp coarse black pepper

Salmon, Prawn &
Scallop Risotto

SERVES 4

**SEAFOOD AND
TOMATO-CAPER SAUCE**

1½ cups canned tomatoes,
chopped but not drained

1½ Tbsp extra-virgin olive oil

1½ Tbsp capers, drained

1½ Tbsp fresh lemon juice

1 Tbsp chopped fresh parsley

¾ tsp kosher salt

¾ tsp coarse black pepper

12 large prawns

12 medium scallops

1 lb skinless, boneless
salmon, in 1-inch chunks

4 vine-ripened tomatoes, in
1½-inch chunks (3 cups)

RISOTTO

2 Tbsp extra-virgin olive oil

½ onion, in ¼-inch
dice (¾ cup)

1 tsp kosher salt

½ tsp coarse black pepper

2 cups arborio rice

2½ cups chicken stock

2½ cups water

½ cup white wine

¾ cup grated Italian
parmesan cheese

4 lemon wedges

TIMING IS EVERYTHING with risotto. Finish up the seafood and tomato-caper sauce just as the risotto is absorbing the last of the liquid, leaving the risotto in its hot pan to keep it warm.

SEAFOOD AND TOMATO-CAPER SAUCE Place canned tomatoes, olive oil, capers, lemon juice, parsley, ¼ tsp of the salt and ¼ tsp of the pepper in a small saucepan and bring to a simmer on medium heat. Remove from the heat as it starts to simmer, and set aside.

RISOTTO Heat olive oil in a saucepan on medium. Add onions, salt and pepper and cook until onions are translucent, 5 to 6 minutes. Stir in rice, chicken stock and ½ of the water and increase the heat to medium-high. Bring to a boil, then reduce the heat to medium and allow to simmer, stirring frequently with a heat-resistant rubber spatula, until rice has absorbed the liquid. Add the remaining water and wine, a little bit at a time, stirring constantly. When the rice is creamy and has absorbed all the liquid, about 25 minutes, mix in parmesan, remove from the heat and set aside.

FINISH SAUCE To the sauce, add prawns, scallops, salmon, fresh tomatoes and the remaining ½ tsp salt and ½ tsp pepper and simmer on medium-low, covered, just until the seafood is cooked, about 3 minutes.

Divide risotto among 4 bowls, flattening the top of each mound a little. Spoon the sauce onto the risotto, arranging the seafood evenly on the top and gathering the prawns with their tails in the air. Garnish with a wedge of lemon and serve immediately.

Prawn Risotto

— WITH CHAMPAGNE SAUCE —

CHAMPAGNE SAUCE

¼ cup unsalted butter

10 shallots, in
¼-inch dice (1¼ cups)

¼ tsp kosher salt

¼ tsp coarse black pepper

1¼ cups whipping cream

1 cup Champagne or good-
quality sparkling white wine

Shells and tails from
16 jumbo prawns

RISOTTO

1 bunch pencil-thin
asparagus (about 12 stalks)

2 Tbsp extra-virgin olive oil

1 onion, in ¼-inch dice
(1½ cups)

1 tsp kosher salt

½ tsp coarse black pepper

2 cups arborio rice

2½ cups chicken stock

2½ cups water

½ cup white wine

¾ cup grated Italian
parmesan cheese

16 jumbo prawns, butterflied

1 vine-ripened tomato,
in ¼-inch dice (¾ cup)

4 lemon wedges

PEEL THE PRAWNS for this recipe ahead of time so that you have shells and tails available to make the sauce.

CHAMPAGNE SAUCE Heat butter in a saucepan on medium. Add shallots, salt and pepper and cook until just translucent, 4 to 5 minutes. Add cream, Champagne and prawn shells and tails and simmer slowly until reduced to 2 cups, about 10 minutes. Strain sauce through a fine-mesh sieve into a clean saucepan. Discard the prawn shells and tails. Cover sauce and set aside.

RISOTTO Cut and discard bottom 2 inches of each asparagus stem. Cut and reserve top 2 inches of each asparagus tip for the sauce. Cut the remaining stems in ⅛-inch slices, no larger! Set aside.

Heat olive oil in a saucepan on medium. Add onions, salt and pepper and cook until onions are translucent, 5 to 6 minutes. Stir in rice, chicken stock and ½ of the water and increase the heat to medium-high. Bring to a boil, then reduce the heat to medium and allow to simmer, stirring frequently with a heat-resistant rubber spatula, until rice has absorbed the liquid. After 15 minutes, add sliced asparagus. Add the remaining water and wine, a little bit at a time, stirring constantly, about 10 minutes more. When the rice is creamy and has absorbed all the liquid, mix in parmesan, remove from the heat and set aside.

FINISH SAUCE To the sauce, add prawns, asparagus tips and tomatoes and cook until prawns just turn opaque and asparagus tips are tender-crisp, 2 to 3 minutes.

Divide risotto among 4 bowls, flattening the top of each mound a little. Spoon the sauce over the risotto, arranging the prawns and asparagus evenly on the top and gathering the prawns with their tails in the air. Garnish with a wedge of lemon and serve immediately.

Teriyaki Chicken Rice Bowl

A WELL-SEASONED WOK or steel frying pan will make all the difference to this recipe. If it has not already been seasoned, wash it with soapy water and dry it thoroughly. Place a few drops of vegetable oil in the pan and wipe them off with a paper towel, leaving only a thin coating. Heat the pan on low, then increase the heat to blue-hot (or medium on an electric stove). Remove the pan from the heat, fill it with table salt and heat it again over a blue-hot flame. Cool, then use a thick tea towel to vigorously rub the salt around the pan. Allow the salt to cool completely and discard it, then wipe clean the pan with a drop of oil. Scramble some eggs. If the eggs stick, rub that spot with a lightly oiled cloth. Use your seasoned pan often but never wash it with soap; use salt instead.

Sugar snap peas are a great substitute for the broccoli in this recipe and do not need blanching. Mirin is a sweet cooking wine, and a common brand is Honteri.

TERIYAKI SAUCE Combine all ingredients in a saucepan on medium heat. Bring to a simmer for 2 minutes, stirring constantly. Will keep refrigerated for up to 5 days.

CHICKEN STIRFRY Bring a medium pot of water to a boil on high heat. Add broccoli and simmer for 30 seconds to blanch them. Remove from the heat, drain and set aside.

Place butter and garlic in a large frying pan on medium-high heat (do not brown the butter). Add chicken and sauté until it is ¼ cooked, about 2 minutes (it will be browned on the outside but still pink inside). Stir in bell peppers, red onions, mushrooms, broccoli and teriyaki sauce. Cook on high heat, shaking the pan, until chicken is just cooked and vegetables are tender-crisp, 3 to 4 minutes. Remove from the heat.

Divide rice among 4 bowls. Top with chicken stirfry, garnish with green onions, and serve immediately.

SERVES 4

TERIYAKI SAUCE
¾ cup low-sodium soy sauce

6 Tbsp mirin

6 Tbsp white wine

6 Tbsp pineapple juice (preferably not from concentrate)

¼ cup brown sugar

½ tsp finely grated fresh ginger

1½ Tbsp cornstarch

CHICKEN STIRFRY
2 cups broccoli florets

2 Tbsp melted unsalted butter

2 tsp minced garlic

1 lb skinless, boneless chicken breasts, in ¼-inch slices

½ green bell pepper, in ½-inch dice (½ cup)

½ red bell pepper, in ½-inch dice (½ cup)

⅓ red onion, in ½-inch dice (½ cup)

½ cup sliced shiitake mushrooms

4 cups freshly cooked jasmine rice

2 green onions, in ⅛-inch diagonal slices (¼ cup)

Salmon Shiitake Rice Bowl

MIRIN, A SWEET cooking rice wine, and dashi (or instant dashi powder), a stock usually made from dried seaweed and dried tuna flakes, are found in many Asian cooking stores. Look for shichimi togarashi, the Japanese 7-spice seasoning mix made with red chili peppers, roasted orange peels, yellow and black sesame seeds, Japanese pepper, seaweed and ginger, at Japanese food stores.

SAKE-DASHI-GINGER BROTH In a small bowl, whisk together water and cornstarch. Combine remaining ingredients in a large pot on medium-high heat. Whisking constantly, add the corn-starch mixture and bring to a boil until thickened. Set aside.

SALMON AND VEGETABLES Heat canola oil in a shallow pan on medium. Add salmon, salt and pepper, and 2 Tbsp of the sake-dashi-ginger broth, cover and pan-fry for about 4 minutes per side. The salmon will start to flake and be slightly pink in the middle. Remove from the heat and set aside.

Bring the remaining sake-dashi-ginger broth to a simmer on medium heat. Add mushrooms, bell peppers and onions and cook until heated through, 2 to 3 minutes. Stir in spinach until just wilted but nice and green.

Divide rice among 4 bowls. Pour vegetables and broth over the rice and top with a piece of salmon. Serve immediately.

SERVES 4

SAKE-DASHI-GINGER BROTH
2¼ cups cold water

2 Tbsp cornstarch

1½ Tbsp dashi

¾ cup mirin

6 Tbsp low-sodium soy sauce

¼ cup sake

2 tsp rice vinegar

4 tsp fresh lemon juice

4 tsp minced garlic

4 tsp finely grated fresh ginger

¼ tsp shichimi togarashi

SALMON AND VEGETABLES
1½ tsp canola oil

4 skinless, boneless salmon fillets, each 4 to 6 oz

½ tsp kosher salt

½ tsp coarse black pepper

⅔ cup sliced shiitake mushrooms

1 red bell pepper, in ½-inch dice (1 cup)

½ red onion, in ¼-inch dice (¾ cup)

6 oz spinach leaves, washed and patted dry

4 cups freshly cooked jasmine rice

Prawn & Lentil Rice Bowl

SERVES 4

ROSE SHALLOT SAUCE

1½ tsp extra-virgin olive oil

2 Tbsp diced onions

2 shallots, in ¼-inch dice (¼ cup)

1 tsp minced garlic

¼ tsp kosher salt

⅛ tsp coarse black pepper

Pinch of crushed chilies

⅛ tsp cayenne pepper

1 dash Tabasco sauce

¾ cup canned tomatoes, chopped but not drained

½ Tbsp chopped fresh basil leaves

½ Tbsp grated Italian parmesan cheese

2 cups whipping cream

½ cup fish stock

Shells and tails from 20 jumbo prawns

PINO POSTERARO, OWNER of Cioppino's Mediterranean Grill and Enoteca, didn't set out to become a chef. In fact he was training to be a heart surgeon when his brother, who owned a restaurant in Toronto, changed his career path. Medicine's loss was the restaurant industry's gain! Pino often uses lentils in his dishes as he enjoys the texture and earthy flavours that they add. This particular dish earned rave reviews from our guests during our Bella Italia promotion!

Peel the prawns ahead of time so that you have shells and tails available to make the sauce.

ROSE SHALLOT SAUCE Heat olive oil in a large saucepan on medium. Add onions, shallots, garlic, salt, pepper, chilies, cayenne and Tabasco sauce and cook until onions are translucent, about 5 minutes. Stir in tomatoes, basil and parmesan. Remove from the heat.

Combine cream, fish stock and prawn shells and tails in a medium saucepan on medium heat. Allow to simmer gently until the liquid is reduced to 1¼ cups, about 20 minutes. Remove and discard prawn shells and tails. Stir the cream mixture into the tomato sauce and bring it to a simmer for 3 minutes. Remove from the heat and set aside.

LENTIL AND VEGETABLE RICE Combine lentils, chicken stock, bay leaf, oregano, thyme, rosemary, sage and basil in a large saucepan on medium-low heat. Cook for 10 minutes, then add celery, carrots, bell peppers, shallots, peas, salt and pepper. Cook for 5 to 7 minutes more, or until lentils are cooked but not mushy. Remove and discard bay leaf.

Using a heat-resistant rubber spatula, fold rice into the lentil mixture. Cover and warm on low heat for 1 minute.

PRAWNS AND VEGETABLES Cut and discard bottom 2 inches of each asparagus stem. Cut asparagus into 1½-inch pieces. Place asparagus in a medium saucepan with bell peppers, mushrooms, prawns and rose shallot sauce and simmer on medium heat until prawns are just cooked, about 3 minutes.

Divide the lentil and vegetable rice among 4 bowls. Arrange the sauce, prawns and asparagus evenly on the top, gathering the prawns with their tails in the air, then garnish with a wedge of lemon and some parsley. Serve immediately.

LENTIL AND VEGETABLE RICE

¾ cup French green lentils

1½ cups chicken stock

1 bay leaf

Pinches of dried oregano, thyme, rosemary, sage, and basil

1 celery stalk, in ¼-inch dice (½ cup)

1 carrot, in ¼-inch dice (½ cup)

½ red bell pepper, in ½-inch dice (½ cup)

2 shallots, in ¼-inch dice (¼ cup)

½ cup frozen peas

¼ tsp kosher salt

¼ tsp coarse black pepper

4 cups freshly cooked jasmine rice

PRAWNS AND VEGETABLES

1 bunch pencil-thin asparagus (about 12 stalks)

1 large red bell pepper, in ½-inch dice

¾ cup sliced mushrooms

20 jumbo prawns, butterflied

4 lemon wedges

2 Tbsp chopped fresh parsley

Sukiyaki Rice Bowl

SERVES 4

SUKIYAKI SAUCE

1¼ cups water

½ cup low-sodium soy sauce

½ cup sake

½ cup mirin

2½ Tbsp pineapple juice (preferably not from concentrate)

3½ Tbsp brown sugar

1 Tbsp dashi

½ tsp shichimi togarashi

½ tsp minced garlic

¼ tsp grated fresh ginger

2 tsp cornstarch

BEEF AND VEGETABLES

1 Tbsp sesame oil

3 Tbsp canola oil

1 lb sirloin steak, in ⅛-inch strips

1 cup sliced shiitake mushrooms

2 shallots, in ¼-inch dice (¼ cup)

2 Tbsp minced garlic

1 Tbsp grated fresh ginger

1 tsp coarse black pepper

½ yellow bell pepper, in ½-inch dice (½ cup)

½ red bell pepper, in ½-inch dice (½ cup)

½ cup sugar snap peas, stemmed and stringed, cut in half on the diagonal

1 cup spinach leaves, washed and patted dry

4 cups cooked jasmine rice

2 green onions, in ⅛-inch slices (¼ cup)

SUKIYAKI IS A Japanese soup or stew prepared hotpot style with thinly sliced beef. Most of the ingredients used to make this rice bowl are available at your local grocery store. Look for mirin, dashi (or instant dashi powder) and shichimi togarashi, the Japanese 7-spice seasoning mix made with red chili peppers, roasted orange peels, yellow and black sesame seeds, Japanese pepper, seaweed and ginger, at Asian food stores.

SUKIYAKI SAUCE Combine all ingredients in a small saucepan until well mixed. Bring to a simmer, stirring constantly, on medium heat for about 5 minutes. Will keep refrigerated for up to 5 days.

BEEF AND VEGETABLES Heat sesame and canola oils in a very large frying pan on very high. Add beef, mushrooms, shallots, garlic, ginger and pepper and sauté very briefly, 1½ to 2 minutes, or just until beef and mushrooms are nicely browned. Move this mixture to 1 side of the pan. Stir in sukiyaki sauce along with bell peppers, peas and spinach. Cover and steam until vegetables are just crisp and hot and the spinach is just wilted and still bright green, 1 to 2 minutes.

Mound rice in the middle of each bowl. Divide the beef and mixed vegetables over the rice and sprinkle with green onions. Serve immediately.

The Toigos
Take the Reins

BY THE 1990S, the foodie movement had begun to sprout. Suddenly, home cooks were acquiring an adventurous spirit with recipes requiring burnt sage butter and sun-dried tomatoes. Cooking shows had gone beyond Julia Child and Jacques Pépin, and younger celebrity chefs like Bobby Flay and Emeril Lagasse came along. TV's *Sex and the City* made the Cosmopolitan cocktail a household name. We were keenly aware of the culinary transformation happening around us. During this period we introduced promotional menus, which gave us the chance to offer our guests something new, without tampering with the tried-and-true White Spot favourites.

The Toigo years have largely been about transitioning a company from old world to new. There were major changes in operations, including the closing down of the old commissary in the '90s. It just

FACING: Peter Toigo Jr. (left) and Ron Toigo (right) with their mom, Elizabeth.

First Franchisee

MICHELE METCALFE-KLETKE was in her early 20s when she was offered the opportunity to become our very first franchisee. She had been working as a server at our Kelowna location, and Michele said she was honoured when she was asked if she'd be interested: "I'm a local girl, born and raised in the Okanagan, and I think the fact that I had already worked my way through White Spot and proven myself as an independent leader and believed in White Spot values, that was a big part of it," says Michele.

"It was a really big deal with White Spot opening in Vernon—tons of people were thrilled." For our Vernon guests, it meant not having to make the drive to Kamloops or Kelowna. Today, half the White Spot locations, including our Triple-O's, are owned by proud franchisees, many of whom pick up awards for excellence at White Spot's annual awards banquet.

Michele spent 16 years with White Spot, including five of them as a franchisee. She gave up the franchise when she started her own family, but she subsequently returned to work as a part-time server at our Kelowna location.

didn't make sense for a rapidly expanding business that had grown beyond the Lower Mainland's borders to run a commissary. Also in the 1990s, we sold off our Kentucky Fried Chicken franchise, choosing to focus on what we do best, which is White Spot.

In March 1993, we opened our first franchise operation, in Vernon, B.C. As most big companies have learned, franchising can be a risky endeavour, but we've gone to lengths to ensure standardization across the board, and it starts with the franchisees themselves. "The key to successful franchising is to find franchisees who love your brand as much as you do," says our President and CEO Warren Erhart. "It's important, because the guest doesn't care if it's a corporate location or a franchise; they just want a great experience. And we have to make sure that the systems are in place to make sure they get treated well."

The Toigos also decided to return White Spot's image to the family-style, down-home comfort-food establishment that had made us hugely successful with British Columbians. Nat Bailey's profile had diminished during the General Foods years, and Warren and the Toigos decided that Nat needed more of a presence, to show our respect. In the 1990s, we put Nat's name in our menus. "I remember Peter Sr. saying that if it weren't for Nat, there wouldn't be a White Spot," says Warren. "He had a great feeling about recognizing the man that he was. And we had some fun bringing him back. He was our Walt Disney." In honour of our founder, we introduced Nat's Hearty Breakfast and Nat Bailey Pale Ale, and we put his picture in our restaurants and in our offices. We even started an incentive program for our top managers, called Nat's All Stars.

"I think the biggest strength of White Spot overall is its people," says Ron Toigo. "Warren is a lot like my dad, to the point where he can walk into a restaurant and know everybody by name. I think people care about that, and as a result, I don't think there's a restaurant anywhere that can compete because we've retained those family values. My father always said, 'The most important guy in the restaurant is the dishwasher. You can run a restaurant without a manager, but try to run it without the guy doing the dishes.' What he meant is everybody has an important role to make the whole thing work, so it doesn't matter what your position is. It's important."

Nat's customer service ethic has stuck with us too, such as treating our guests the way we

The logo on our Nat Bailey Pale Ale glasses shows how Nat's presence was brought to life in our restaurants. The illustration features Nat and his favourite pastime—baseball.

would in our own homes. Peter Jr. says, "We are firm believers that whether you're part of a baseball team or in the trenches in a war, whatever you are doing, you're only as good as the people you've got on the front lines." And if you're not proud of the product, you don't serve it. We have signs in our restaurants that say just that.

Training is a big part of ensuring the values and culture at White Spot, and we teach a class called Legendary Service to all our managers. As part of the workshop, we teach our managers to think "guest first," as in, going the extra mile to ensure that our guests leave feeling not just satisfied but uplifted by the experience. Our success depends on our guests making us a part of their lives and spreading the word about their love for our food and experiences in our restaurants. We don't see our guests as one-time visitors. We see them as valued guests who will be visiting again and again. This idea is a vital part of our training program, and as part of the initiation we tell stories about our history, our people and our guests—like the story of "110 Per Cent Bill." Warren says, "He'd come in every day and you'd ask him, 'How's it going, Bill?' And he'd raise his thumb and say, '110 per cent!'

"Well, Bill passed away, which was sad. And then one day, his son comes in and gives us a cheque to throw a staff party." We'd had such a profound effect on Bill that his son wanted to show the staff his heartfelt appreciation, which touched us all. "What we do is admirable and important, and we can look after people and change their day."

A big part of the modern-era White Spot is our quick-service brand called Triple-O's. In the late '90s, downtown Vancouver real estate prices, particularly on Robson Street, were at an all-time high. Instead of operating a

Nat Bailey's commitment to the highest quality. This sign is still posted in our restaurants today.

Closing the Deal with a Burger and a Shake

BUSINESSMAN JIM PATTISON is as much a B.C. legend as White Spot. His parents took him to our original location at 67th and Granville for regular post-church meals when he was a kid, and when he grew up and married his childhood sweetheart, Mary, Jim took his kids there too. And when he started to grow his car sales business, he'd treat customers who'd just purchased a car by taking them to White Spot.

"I would buy them a hamburger with dill pickle, French fries and a chocolate milkshake," says Jim, for whom the Legendary Burger, fries and chocolate milkshake have been his own standing order his entire life. He doesn't even open the menu.

"You talk about legend, White Spot is a legend. I don't think White Spot used to be any better than it is today. And I certainly want to give credit to Peter C. Toigo and the family. They didn't try to change too much. They kept the tradition and they kept modernizing it and improving it. They deserve a lot of credit for keeping the legacy the way it is. The key is, modernizing the product and the menus. And the product is always excellent."

Was ownership of White Spot ever on Jim's bucket list? Again, he doesn't miss a beat. "A hundred times—I would love to have bought White Spot," he says, smiling. "But I think it's in good hands."

full-service restaurant in that location, it made sense to cater to the heavy tourist and local shopping traffic by offering a White Spot burger concept. "That was an exciting expansion," remembers our Vice President of Human Resources, Denise Buchanan. "It was an evolution. Peter and Warren would meet all the time to talk about their vision of what Triple-O's should be."

We knew that a streamlined menu featuring our bestsellers would be a surefire way to please guests who were on the go. "It was based upon what we call our 'hero products,'" says Warren. "Burgers, fries and shakes. And we wanted a retro diner feel to it." In 1997, we opened our first Triple-O's on a smaller footprint in the heart of the Robson and Thurlow shopping hub.

The model was so successful that Arthur Griffiths, the owner of what was then known as GM Place, asked us to open one there, to serve sports and music fans. We now have three kiosks at what is today called Rogers Arena.

"Really, what made it work was our partnership with Chevron," says Ron Toigo. That partnership gave us a convenient presence at gas stations where our guests could make a pit stop for our Legendary Burgers and fries. "Chevron has the same ideology. They never cut corners. Their commitment to excellence was the same. We joined with them to build the Triple-O's concept and opened 10 restaurants overnight; from there the brand never looked back. It's really been a growth vehicle that we never anticipated. It's probably our best

Employees from all our Lower Mainland locations gathered for a portrait during White Spot's 65th anniversary celebrations in 1993. Longtime employee Joe Scianna is fourth from the right, standing.

innovation since we owned the company. It's gone very well because the quality is second to none." The Triple-O's brand now serves millions of guests a year.

While our quick-service Triple-O's with the limited menu harkened back to Nat's first food-cart service and fulfilled the niche for ease and convenience, our full-service restaurants were poised to change. Our guests started to become more health conscious and open to culinary adventure, and in order to realize Nat's dream of longevity and expansion, we knew our next step would be an overall transformation.

The first Triple-O's location opened in Vancouver at Robson and Thurlow in 1997.

Entrées

Bishop's Chicken Curry

SERVES 4

CURRY SAUCE

¼ cup melted unsalted butter

⅛ tsp cinnamon

¼ tsp garam masala

¼ tsp turmeric

¼ tsp ground cardamom

¼ tsp ground coriander

1 bay leaf

⅛ tsp crushed chilies

1 tsp kosher salt

½ onion, in ¼-inch dice (¾ cup)

1 Tbsp minced garlic

2 tsp grated fresh ginger

1 cup canned tomatoes, puréed

¼ cup ground almonds

1 cup coconut milk

¼ cup chicken stock

¼ cup whipping cream

1 Tbsp fresh lime juice

CHICKEN CURRY

1 lb skinless, boneless chicken breasts, in ¼-inch slices

½ yellow bell pepper, in ½-inch dice (½ cup)

½ red bell pepper, in ½-inch dice (½ cup)

½ cup sugar snap peas, stemmed and stringed, cut in half on the diagonal

1 Granny Smith apple, in ½-inch dice (½ cup)

4 cups cooked jasmine rice

½ cup mango chutney

20 sprigs fresh cilantro leaves, held in water and patted dry before use

JOHN BISHOP OPENED his restaurant on West Fourth Avenue in Vancouver in 1985, which was inspired by his love of fresh local produce, classic but innovative cooking and friendly yet professional service. He was one of the original champions of Pacific Northwest cooking.

This recipe, which was developed with John for our Celebrate BC promotion, has become a favourite with our guests. Of his experience as one of our celebrity chefs, John says, "I've enjoyed it. I'm very complimented that they used my recipes." Serve this curry with naan bread that's been coated lightly with butter and heated in the oven or toasted on the barbecue.

CURRY SAUCE Heat butter in a large saucepan on medium. Add cinnamon, garam masala, turmeric, cardamom, coriander, bay leaf, chilies and salt and sauté for 2 minutes to develop their aroma. Stir in onions, garlic and ginger and cook until onions are translucent, about 5 minutes. Add tomatoes, almonds, coconut milk, chicken stock, cream and lime juice and simmer, covered, for 30 minutes to allow flavours to blend. Remove and discard bay leaf.

CHICKEN CURRY Place chicken, bell peppers, snap peas and apples in a large saucepan with the curry sauce. Simmer on medium-high heat until chicken is just cooked, about 5 minutes.

Divide rice among 4 bowls. Pour curry over the rice and garnish with generous spoonfuls of mango chutney and several sprigs of cilantro. Serve immediately.

Chicken Pot Pie

SERVES 4

¼ cup butter

½ onion, in ½-inch dice (¾ cup)

2 shallots, in ¼-inch dice (¼ cup)

1 tsp minced garlic

1 tsp kosher salt

½ tsp coarse black pepper

½ tsp chopped fresh rosemary

½ tsp chopped fresh thyme

¼ tsp chopped fresh sage

¼ cup all-purpose flour

1¼ cups chicken stock

4 tsp sherry

¼ tsp Worcestershire sauce

1 skinless, boneless chicken breast + 2 skinless, boneless chicken thighs, 7 oz total

1 carrot, in ¼-inch dice (½ cup)

1 medium red potato, in ½-inch dice (½ cup)

1½ celery stalks, in ¼-inch dice (¾ cup)

1 bay leaf

½ cup frozen peas

⅓ cup whipping cream

1 Tbsp chopped fresh parsley

1 pkg frozen puff pastry

1 large egg, beaten

1 Tbsp milk

AN ALL-TIME CLASSIC Comfort Food dish! It can be prepared using four individual ovenproof bowls or family style in a large casserole dish. Serve with a garden salad.

MELT butter in a large pot on medium heat. Add onions, shallots and garlic and season with salt, pepper, rosemary, thyme and sage. Cook until onions and shallots are translucent, about 7 minutes. Stir in flour and cook for another 5 minutes, or until this roux is blond and smells nutty.

Gradually stir in chicken stock, sherry and Worcestershire sauce. Allow the mixture to come to a simmer. Reduce the heat to medium-low, then add chicken, carrots, potatoes, celery and bay leaf and simmer, covered, for 20 to 30 minutes until the carrots are soft. Mix in peas, cream and parsley and allow the mixture to return to a simmer for 2 more minutes. Remove from the heat and set aside.

Preheat the oven to 400°F. Remove and discard the bay leaf from the chicken mixture, then ladle the hot chicken mixture into 4 ovenproof soup bowls (or a large casserole dish, if you want to serve this dish family style). Set the bowls (or the casserole dish) on a baking sheet.

On a clean work surface, roll out puff pastry to about ⅛ inch thick (each pastry should be large enough in diameter to extend ½ inch past the edge of the soup bowl or casserole dish). To make an egg wash, combine egg and milk in a small bowl. Brush puff pastry on 1 side with the egg wash, and place egg wash side down over each bowl or the casserole dish. Fold the edges of the puff pastry down the side of each bowl or the casserole dish to completely encase the chicken mixture. Brush the top side of each puff pastry with egg wash and bake for 12 to 15 minutes, or until the pastry rises, becomes dark golden brown and crisps slightly. Serve immediately.

Chicken Gai Yang

THIS DISH WAS developed for our Taste of Thai promotion with Jareuk Sri-Arun, a celebrated Thai chef and instructor at the Suan Dusit International Culinary School in Bangkok. To ensure the dishes for this promotion were authentic, our Executive Chef, Chuck Currie, travelled to Thailand to work with Jareuk, who believes that the preparation of the ingredients is as essential to the final taste of the dish as the quality of the ingredients themselves. Gai yang means "barbecued (or grilled) chicken" and is a common street food in Thailand that can be prepared in many different ways. We prefer the Mae Ploy brand of curry paste, which is available in many Asian markets. Look for sambal oelek, the puréed Indonesian hot pepper sauce, and ketjap manis, the sweet Indonesian soy sauce, while you're there. Serve this dish with rice.

PEANUT SAUCE Combine all ingredients in a food processor and purée until smooth. Will keep refrigerated for up to 3 days.

CUCUMBER RELISH In a small saucepan on medium heat, bring sugar, vinegar and salt to a boil. Remove from the heat and allow to cool to room temperature. Stir in cucumbers, shallots and chilies and refrigerate for about 1 hour before using. Will keep refrigerated for up to 1 day.

THAI RED CURRY SAUCE Heat canola oil in a large frying pan on medium. Using a heat-resistant rubber spatula, mix in curry paste until totally combined with the oil. (The curry paste will want to stick to the bottom of the saucepan; allow it to cook and colour slightly before scraping it off but keep working at it consistently for a few minutes.) The paste will darken and become very aromatic.

Stir in coconut milk, continuing to scrape the curry paste from the bottom of the saucepan with the rubber spatula, then bring to a simmer without stirring, allowing the coconut fat to break from the sauce. Pour in fish sauce, brown sugar and lime juice, continuing to stir the mixture until sugar dissolves. Cover and set aside. *continued overleaf >*

SERVES 4

PEANUT SAUCE
¼ cup smooth peanut butter

1½ Tbsp water

1 Tbsp rice vinegar

1 tsp sambal oelek

1 Tbsp ketjap manis

¼ tsp minced garlic

¼ tsp finely grated fresh ginger

2 Tbsp chopped fresh cilantro

CUCUMBER RELISH
¼ cup granulated sugar

2 Tbsp rice vinegar

¼ tsp kosher salt

¼ English cucumber, in ⅜-inch dice (½ cup)

1 shallot, in ⅛-inch slices (2 Tbsp)

1 pickled Thai bird's eye chili, finely sliced

THAI RED CURRY SAUCE
1 Tbsp canola oil

5 Tbsp Thai red curry paste

2 cups coconut milk

2 Tbsp fish sauce

3 Tbsp brown sugar

2 Tbsp fresh lime juice

CHICKEN GAI YANG
4 Gai Yang-Marinated
Chicken breasts (page 67)

½ cup diced fresh pineapple

2 green onions, in ⅛-inch
diagonal slices (¼ cup)

½ cup sliced mushrooms

½ red bell pepper,
in ¼-inch dice (½ cup)

1 cup bean sprouts

12 sprigs fresh cilantro
leaves, held in water and
patted dry before use

CHICKEN GAI YANG Preheat the barbecue to medium. Remove chicken breasts from the marinade and place them on the grill. Rotate chicken breasts after a minute so that they don't stick and so that they become marked with nice crossed grill marks. Flip the chicken after 4 minutes, and cook for another 4 minutes, rotating the meat on the grill. To test for doneness, poke along the grain with your tongs at the thickest point. The juices should run clear and the meat should be opaque. (If you have a meat thermometer, the internal temperature should read at least 165°F.) Remove from the heat and set aside.

Return the frying pan with the Thai red curry sauce to medium heat and add the pineapple, green onions, mushrooms and bell peppers. Simmer for 2 to 3 minutes, or until peppers are cooked but still crisp. Add bean sprouts and toss until heated through but still crisp.

Divide curry sauce and vegetables among 4 bowls, then top each serving with a chicken breast. Drizzle with lines of peanut sauce. Place a dollop of cucumber relish on each chicken breast and sprinkle cilantro leaves around the perimeter of the bowl. Serve immediately.

Executive Chef Chuck Currie with Chef Jareuk Sri-Arun at a spice market in Thailand, 2007.

Curried Broccoli & Chicken Casserole

A GUEST FAVOURITE AND classic White Spot dish. Serve this casserole with rice and salad.

IN A LARGE saucepan on medium-low heat, cook shallots in 2 Tbsp of the butter with the salt, pepper, garlic, curry powder and nutmeg until translucent, about 5 minutes. Add the mushrooms, increase the heat to medium and cook until just soft, 4 to 5 minutes. Remove from the heat.

In a food processor, purée ⅔ of the mushroom mixture, leaving the remaining mushrooms in the pan. Return the puréed mushrooms to the pan and stir well to combine. On low heat, add flour and cook, stirring, for 10 minutes. Gradually stir in chicken stock, cream and lemon juice. Increase the heat to medium and allow the mixture to come to a simmer. Add chicken and broccoli and simmer, covered, for 5 minutes to just barely cook the broccoli. Remove from the heat and set aside.

Preheat the oven to 400°F. Stir mayonnaise into the casserole and transfer the mixture to a 9 × 12-inch ovenproof casserole dish. Cover with the cheeses.

In a small bowl, combine the remaining 4 Tbsp butter and bread crumbs until well mixed and sprinkle over the casserole. Bake for 15 to 20 minutes, or until the internal temperature is 165°F and the bread crumbs are nicely browned with the liquid bubbling at the edges. Serve immediately.

SERVES 4

3 shallots, in ¼-inch dice (6 Tbsp)

6 Tbsp melted butter

½ tsp kosher salt

¼ tsp coarse black pepper

½ tsp minced garlic

2 tsp Madras curry powder

Pinch of nutmeg

1 cup sliced mushrooms

2 Tbsp all-purpose flour

1¼ cups chicken stock

½ cup whipping cream

1 tsp fresh lemon juice

1 lb skinless, boneless chicken breasts, in ¼-inch slices

4 cups broccoli florets

½ cup mayonnaise

1 cup shredded medium cheddar cheese

1 cup shredded mozzarella cheese

1 cup bread crumbs

Halibut with Black Bean Sauce

THIS RECIPE WAS developed for our Celebrate BC promotion with celebrity chef John Bishop. Find fermented black beans, oyster sauce, and sambal oelek, a puréed Indonesian hot pepper sauce, at Asian markets or your local grocery store. Substitute ¼ cup store-bought fermented black bean sauce if you prefer not to soak and chop the whole beans yourself. Serve this dish over rice.

HEAT chicken (or fish) stock, black beans, oyster sauce, sesame oil, ginger, sugar, sambal oelek and garlic in a medium nonstick saucepan on medium-high heat and bring to a simmer.

In a small bowl, whisk together sherry, rice vinegar and cornstarch, then whisk into the simmering sauce. Continue whisking until the sauce returns to a simmer. Increase the heat to high.

To the sauce, add halibut, bok choy, peas, leeks and carrots and cook for 2 to 3 minutes until halibut is just done (it will flake with a fork) and vegetables are tender-crisp. Divide among 4 plates or serve family style, garnished with green onions.

SERVES 4

1 cup chicken or fish stock

2 Tbsp Asian fermented black beans, soaked in very hot water for 5 minutes, drained and chopped

5 Tbsp oyster sauce

1½ tsp sesame oil

1½ tsp finely grated fresh ginger

1 Tbsp granulated sugar

2 tsp sambal oelek

2 tsp minced garlic

1 Tbsp sherry

4 tsp rice vinegar

1¼ tsp cornstarch

1 lb skinless, boneless halibut, in 1-inch pieces

2 cups baby bok choy, stemmed

½ cup sugar snap peas, stemmed and stringed

¼ to ½ leek (white and light green parts only), sliced (½ cup)

1 carrot, in ¼-inch slices (½ cup)

3 green onions, in ¼-inch diagonal slices (⅜ cup)

Fish & Chips

SERVES 4

TARTAR SAUCE

1 Tbsp capers,
drained and chopped

1 Tbsp chopped dill pickles

1 shallot, in ¼-inch
dice (1 Tbsp)

1 Tbsp chopped fresh parsley

1 tsp chopped fresh dill

1 cup mayonnaise

2 Tbsp fresh lemon juice

¼ tsp coarse black pepper

⅛ tsp kosher salt

FISH AND CHIPS

2 cups all-purpose flour

½ cup cornstarch

2 cups soda water

1½ tsp kosher salt

1½ tsp baking powder

1 lb skinless, boneless
halibut or cod fillets, in 8
pieces, each 3 × 2 × ½ inch

¼ tsp kosher salt

¼ tsp coarse black pepper

1 recipe French
Fries (page 38)

4 lemon wedges

A WHITE SPOT CLASSIC! Do not attempt this dish if you do not have a good-quality home deep fryer. Heating oil in a pot on an open stove without good thermostatic control is very dangerous.

Make the tartar sauce the day before you plan to serve it so that the flavours have time to meld. And cook up a batch of oven-baked French fries from our poutine recipe (page 38) without the cheese and beef gravy, while you prepare the fish.

TARTAR SAUCE Combine all ingredients until well mixed, cover and refrigerate overnight. Will keep refrigerated for up to 3 days.

FISH AND CHIPS Preheat the deep fryer to 350°F. While the fryer is warming up, combine flour, cornstarch, soda water, salt and baking powder until well mixed. Transfer to a shallow bowl and set aside.

Line a plate with paper towels. Season halibut (or cod) with salt and pepper. Using tongs, dip 1 piece at a time in the batter, then hold it in the deep fryer for 15 seconds to allow the batter to set before adding the next piece. Continue until all the fish is cooking. Remove halibut (or cod) after 3 minutes and set aside on the paper towel–lined plate.

Divide French fries among 4 plates and top each serving with a piece of fish. Serve with a side of tartar sauce and a wedge of lemon.

Liver & Onions

JOHN BISHOP, THE celebrated Vancouver restaurateur, discovered White Spot shortly after he came to Canada from the U.K. in 1973. He'd often buy his groceries from a shop around the corner from his home and near our restaurant, and, being a Brit, he was delighted to find liver and onions on our menu. He soon became a regular guest and found he loved the Legendary Burger and the whole diner experience too. Many years later, John appeared in several of our TV commercials, helping us put a face to the growing local food scene.

The secret to cooking liver beautifully is to buy very young calf's liver and to sear it very briefly over very high heat. Searing the meat prevents the juices from escaping and keeps the inside of the liver slightly pink, not grey. Use high heat bravely and briefly.

WARM 4 plates and a platter in the oven. Heat 2 Tbsp of the olive oil and 1 Tbsp of the butter in a large nonstick frying pan on high. When the butter foams, add onions and ¼ tsp of the salt and cook until the onions release their juices, about 5 minutes. Reduce the heat to medium and continue to cook until lightly browned and sticky, 10 to 12 minutes longer. Transfer the onions to a medium bowl and set aside.

Set the pan back on the stove and increase the heat to very high. Season the liver on both sides with pepper and the remaining ¼ tsp salt. To the pan, add the remaining 1 Tbsp olive oil and 2 Tbsp butter. They should be shimmering with heat. Add liver and sage and cook for just 1 to 1½ minutes. The edges of the liver should be just brown. Turn the liver over and cook the other side for 1 to 1½ minutes. Remove from the heat immediately. Transfer liver to the warmed platter.

To the liver juices in the pan, add the reserved onions, lemon juice and parsley. Sauté on medium heat for 1 to 1½ minutes, then divide mixture among the 4 warmed plates. Top with cooked liver. Serve immediately.

SERVES 4

3 Tbsp extra-virgin olive oil

3 Tbsp melted butter

3 onions, in ⅛-inch slices (4½ cups)

½ tsp kosher salt

1½ lbs calf's liver, ⅜ inch thick

¼ tsp coarse black pepper

6 fresh sage leaves

2 Tbsp fresh lemon juice

2 Tbsp chopped fresh parsley

Meatloaf

MUSHROOM GRAVY MAKES a great accompaniment to this meatloaf. We use beer in our recipe—pale ale works best. Prepare the mushroom gravy ahead of time so that it is ready to serve when the meatloaf is cooked.

MUSHROOM GRAVY Melt butter in a medium frying pan on high heat, add mushrooms, onions, garlic, mustard, salt and pepper and cook until nicely browned, 5 to 10 minutes. Pour in beer and vinegar and scrape the bottom pan with a wooden spoon to release any glazed juices or browned bits of mushrooms and onions. Stir in beef gravy and bring to a simmer, then reduce the heat to low and cover. Simmer gravy for 10 minutes to allow flavours to combine.

MEATLOAF Preheat the oven to 350°F. Grease a 9 × 5-inch loaf pan with cooking spray.

Cook bacon in a small pan on medium heat until crisp, about 5 minutes. Pour off fat, reserving 1 Tbsp in the pan. Add onions, garlic, thyme, salt, pepper, mustard, Worcestershire sauce and Tabasco sauce and cook until onions are just translucent, about 6 minutes.

Transfer the onion mixture to a large bowl. Add eggs, milk, ground meats, oats and parsley and mix until just combined nicely.

Turn the meat mixture into the loaf pan, pat into place, cover with aluminum foil and bake for about 1 hour. (If you have a meat thermometer, the internal temperature should read at least 165°F.) Allow to rest for 10 minutes, then cut into 8 slices. Place 2 slices on each plate, ladle ½ cup over gravy overtop and serve immediately.

SERVES 4

MUSHROOM GRAVY

1 Tbsp butter

1⅓ cups sliced mushrooms (about 16 mushrooms)

½ onion, in ¼-inch dice (¾ cup)

1 tsp minced garlic

1½ tsp grainy Dijon mustard

½ tsp kosher salt

½ tsp coarse black pepper

¾ cup beer

1 Tbsp balsamic vinegar

2 cups (1 recipe) Beef Gravy (page 38)

MEATLOAF

½ lb bacon, in 1-inch dice

1 onion, in ¼-inch dice (1½ cups)

1 Tbsp minced garlic

½ tsp dried thyme

1 tsp kosher salt

½ tsp coarse black pepper

2 tsp grainy Dijon mustard

2 tsp Worcestershire sauce

¼ tsp Tabasco sauce

2 large eggs

¼ cup milk

1½ lbs lean ground beef

½ lb ground pork

½ cup rolled oats

⅓ cup chopped fresh parsley

KANSAS CITY–STYLE
Baby Back Ribs

SERVES 6

BABY BACK RIBS

2 Tbsp butter

½ onion, in ¼-inch
dice (¾ cup)

1 Tbsp minced garlic

1½ tsp chili powder

1½ tsp kosher salt

½ tsp coarse black pepper

2 cups tomato juice

¾ cup malt vinegar

2 Tbsp Worcestershire sauce

1 Tbsp minced chipotle
chilies in adobo sauce

2 Tbsp molasses

½ tsp mustard powder

6 baby back ribs, each 1 lb

2 cups beef stock

BBQ SPICE RUB

2 Tbsp paprika

1 Tbsp chili powder

1 Tbsp brown sugar

1 Tbsp kosher salt

1½ tsp dried oregano

1½ tsp granulated sugar

1½ tsp coarse black pepper

¾ tsp cayenne pepper

THIS CLASSIC COOKING style consists of piling ribs together on the barbecue over fairly low heat for a couple of hours so the dry heat develops their flavour while the moist heat from marinating the ribs steams and tenderizes them. Start making this dish one day ahead to allow for marinating overnight. Multiplying this recipe increases the fun and flavour! Look for chipotle chilies in adobo sauce in the Mexican food section of most grocery stores.

BABY BACK RIBS Melt butter in a large frying pan on medium heat. Add onions, garlic, chili powder, salt and pepper and cook until onions are just soft and not browned, about 5 minutes. Pour in tomato juice, vinegar, Worcestershire sauce, chipotle chilies in adobo sauce, molasses and mustard powder and bring to a simmer for 5 minutes, stirring occasionally. Remove from the heat and allow to cool to room temperature.

Place marinade in a large resealable plastic bag, add baby back ribs, close tightly and marinate overnight in the refrigerator.

BBQ SPICE RUB In a bowl, mix all ingredients until well blended.

FINISH RIBS Preheat the oven to 375 °F. Remove ribs from the marinade (reserving this liquid to make a sauce for the ribs) and rub BBQ spice rub all over them with your hands. Place in a large 2-inch-deep, 12-inch square baking pan (the ribs should not protrude from the pan). Set aside.

To make the sauce, simmer marinade in a small saucepan on medium heat until thickened, no more than 10 minutes.

To the ribs, add beef stock, cover tightly with aluminum foil and bake for 2 hours.

Preheat 1 side of a gas barbecue to medium-low. Remove ribs from oven and pile them on the unlit side of the barbecue. Remember, the bigger the pile of ribs, the better the eating!

The ribs will not cook over direct heat, so don't worry about the bottom ones burning. Crack open the base and lid louvers of the barbecue just a ½ inch so you get a low temperature, about 300 °F (if you have a smoker with your barbecue, all the better). Cook for 2 to 2½ hours … the longer you cook the ribs, the more tender they'll be. Now tie on your bib and dig in.

Braised Short Ribs

SERVES 4

FOR THIS RECIPE, we use four racks, each 1½ to 2 inches wide and containing four bones, but any combination will work. This makes a lot of ribs, but the leftovers taste even better the following day, and it's a spectacular comfort meal at any time of year.

Serve these short ribs over a hearty bed of risotto, polenta or mashed potatoes with a garden salad, or serve them with seasonal vegetables. Some nice crusty artisan bread to dip in the sauce is mighty nice, too!

MUSHROOM SAUCE In a medium pot, cook bacon in butter on medium heat until bacon is almost crisp, about 3 minutes. Add shallots, garlic, pepper, thyme and portobello mushrooms and cook until shallots are just translucent and mushrooms lightly browned, about 4 minutes. Stir in flour and cook until lightly browned, about 10 minutes. Gradually stir in beef stock, red wine and tomatoes. Allow the mixture to come to a boil. Add porcini mushrooms and simmer, covered, for 20 minutes. Remove from the heat and set aside.

BRAISED SHORT RIBS Preheat the oven to 350 ° F. Season short ribs with salt and pepper. Place canola oil in a heavy-bottomed, ovenproof pot, set on very high heat and add short ribs. Brown well on all sides, about 5 minutes total. Pour in red wine and scrape the bottom of the pan with a wooden spoon to deglaze it. Add mushroom sauce and allow to come to a simmer. Remove from the heat, cover the pot with aluminum foil, then put the lid on. The foil helps seal the pot securely. Cook in the oven for about 2¾ hours, or until the meat is so tender that it almost falls off the bone, but not quite!

Divide the ribs among 4 plates and pour about ½ cup of the mushroom sauce over each serving.

MUSHROOM SAUCE

1 slice thick-cut bacon, in ¼-inch dice

2 Tbsp melted butter

4 shallots, in ¼-inch dice (½ cup)

½ tsp minced garlic

½ tsp coarse black pepper

¼ tsp dried thyme

1 portobello mushroom, stem removed, and cap halved and cut in ¼-inch slices

2 Tbsp all-purpose flour

2 cups beef stock

¼ cup red wine

1 cup canned tomatoes, puréed

8 slices dried porcini mushrooms

BRAISED SHORT RIBS

2½ to 3 lbs short ribs

1½ tsp kosher salt

1½ tsp coarse black pepper

2 Tbsp canola oil

¼ cup red wine

Taking It Up a Notch

THE NEW CENTURY has brought a return to old-time values and old-world memories. With the emphasis on hearth and home, comfort foods such as chicken pot pie and mac 'n' cheese are in demand again, and sustainability has become the buzzword. With it has come a return to basics with organic farming and the local-is-best food movement. Families are looking for casual dining that fits the family budget. Because we've always valued basics such as affordable dining and comfort food, White Spot has remained in lockstep with the times.

To start, we had to adapt to an increasingly competitive marketplace where casual dining had become a boom industry, with other chain restaurants appealing to a young market willing to pay more for menu items and cocktails amid a more upscale décor. It soon became

FACING: Celebrity chef Umberto Menghi with our Executive Chef, Chuck Currie, during the filming of our Taste of Tuscany TV commercial in 2006.

The Story of Triple "O" Sauce

THERE ARE a handful of people who know what's in our Triple "O" sauce, the legendary condiment that goes back to our very first burgers. Because the sauce is prepared off-site, our staff don't even know. Oh, there are theories. Some people think it's as simple as mayonnaise and relish, or Thousand Island dressing and relish. One of the stranger theories on the Internet is that it contains pickle juice.

But we're not talking. Even members of our staff who do know the recipe aren't talking. We can say that after several decades of making Triple "O" sauce, there are a lot of ingredients that go into it.

clear that our strength would be our legacy as a B.C. institution with family appeal. We saw that we could fulfill the demand for lower prices and a family-friendly décor and still serve young guests who'd been raised on our Pirate Paks and now craved our burger platters. We took a long, hard look at our operation, and by 2000, we set about giving ourselves an extreme makeover.

First off, we updated our restaurants' décor with a warm, West Coast ambience, making it the sort of place where families, groups of friends and couples on dates could sink into our booths for a truly laid-back dining experience. We channelled a Whistler feel, incorporating timber beams, river rock and water features into our finishes and offering separate lounge areas to enhance the social experience.

Next, we needed to adapt our menu to modern tastes but without disappointing our tremendously loyal guests. Enter Chuck Currie as our Executive Chef. Chuck had been working for many years with another popular restaurant chain, and he had the know-how to oversee a major food operation as well as the training of its chefs. His first assignment was to give us feedback on our menu. What did he think?

"The single biggest thing I did was simplify the menu," says Chuck. He never changed our famous burgers and sandwiches; instead, he focused on the entrées, changing about 50 ingredients and dropping 30 dishes that weren't selling so well. Over the course of a year, he then set about developing 14 new menu items, such as Spicy Cantonese Chicken Stirfry, Blackened Cajun Chicken and Salmon Primavera.

"There was a lot of work done behind the scenes," says Cathy Tostenson, our Vice President of Marketing and Menu Development. "The menu took on a significant change. We will always honour what our brand stands for, and burgers are at the heart of our DNA. But we needed to respond to evolving consumer eating trends, which meant adding more salads, pasta and chicken dishes. Consumers have changed."

Meanwhile, we realized our public persona needed a transformation too. Nat may have started off selling BBQ chicken, and it may have been a mainstay throughout the '50s and '60s, but for our new demographic, the old chicken logo simply didn't make sense. "We were at a focus group in Calgary," recalls Warren Erhart. "And one of the participants looked at the logo and said, 'What's the chicken for?'"

It was a difficult decision to let go of that iconic old logo, but we had to be honest—it belonged to a bygone era. By Remembrance Day 2003, we unveiled our new brand identity on all our signs, a modern take on a legendary establishment that reflected today's White Spot. We also launched Chuck's first revised menu that fall, and we got instant results. Sales increased. Our guests were happy. It was a win-win.

For decades, a chicken was part of the White Spot logo. The iconic chicken with the spoon and fork originated in the 1960s and was featured until the spring of 2003, when today's logo was unveiled at the opening of our Port Coquitlam, B.C., location.

c. 1993–2003

2003–today

With the more sophisticated menu items, we had to raise the bar and improve the skill levels in our kitchen. To train our chefs to this high level we became involved with the nationally recognized Red Seal Program. But instead of sending our chefs out for training, we decided we'd devise an in-house apprenticeship program. Chuck had the idea, and everyone in the company embraced it. Denise Buchanan, our Vice President of Human Resources, led the way, with the expertise of James Kennedy, a certified Chef de Cuisine and our newly hired Corporate Training Chef. With the support of the Industry Training Authority and go2, which offers training for the B.C. tourism and hospitality industry, our in-house program became the first of its kind—a pioneering way to offer comprehensive and standardized training that would only have been available at post-secondary institutions.

"We've raised the profile of the Red Seal Program substantially," says James. "We are a private restaurant accredited to deliver Red Seal training, in-house, and we are the first restaurant in Canada that has taken that on. It's a huge step for the industry and a real bonus for our high-performing chefs." We now have the biggest on-the-job restaurant in-house training program for chefs in Western Canada. It's a three-year process, involving classroom hours and on-the-job hours, but "it's been a huge boon," says James. "It has improved quality and consistency and has helped us to not only retain our leaders but to attract strong new hires as well."

Ron Toigo adds, "You need consistency. Our guests expect that their favourite White Spot dish will taste the same whether they eat at a restaurant in Vancouver or Campbell River or New Westminster or at any of our

Our state-of-the-art Culinary Centre at our home office in Vancouver, where we train Red Seal chefs.

locations." With the revamped menu, renovated restaurants, new logo and revitalized chefs and new hires, we were ready to launch a bold new advertising campaign to get the word out, and we chose Chuck for the job. In 2005, we introduced Chuck to the public with our Celebrity Chef campaign, featuring well-known local chefs—all of them already White Spot regulars. Our first "Fresh Thinking. Fresh Cooking" ads included local institution John Bishop and Rob Feenie, who was fresh from his win on the Food Network's *Iron Chef America*. A year later, we brought Umberto Menghi on board, and in 2007 we sent Chuck to Thailand to work with Jareuk Sri-Arun to develop our Taste of Thai promotion. In 2009, Gold Medal Canadian Culinary Champion Melissa Craig became a member of the team, and Pino Posteraro, of Cioppino's fame, joined us in 2010 for our Bella Italia promotion.

The TV ads also featured White Spot Red Seal chefs, kitchen staff and servers playing themselves, so the shoots were a down-home experience. We wanted to convey that we are about food,

Our Corporate Training Chef, James Kennedy, with Red Seal chefs Calvin Canlas, Jennifer Moyou and Leo Canapi at our Celebrate BC TV shoot in 2012.

Executive Chef
Chuck Currie
(second from left)
with celebrity chefs
John Bishop (left),
Umberto Menghi
(second from right)
and Rob Feenie
(right) at our 2007
TV shoot.

and that the kitchen is the heart of our business in contrast to our competitors' focus on the front of the house, or dining area. The positive reaction was instant. The campaign generated a lot of buzz. In an economic climate where the full-service restaurant industry was in decline, White Spot's growth in revenue was the exception.

Today, every dish we serve has to earn its way onto our menu. It's a huge effort that involves our chefs, our marketing team, our menu development team, our supply management team, our Culinary Council of in-house taste testers, and of course, our guests. "We constantly monitor sales stats, research food and consumer trends and keep an eye on what our competitors are doing, both here in Canada and in the U.S., to identify areas of opportunity for our menu and promotions. Every dish that appears on our menu goes through a rigorous menu development process," says Cathy Tostenson.

Chuck, along with our Executive Development Chef, Danny Markowicz, brainstorm recipe ideas and work closely with our supply management team to source quality ingredients. It's routine for Danny and Chuck to get together in the kitchen and just cook up a storm. The final dishes are then presented to our Culinary Council, a panel of taste testers from different company departments as well as restaurant managers and Red Seal chefs. Once a dish gets a thumbs-up from the Culinary Council, we choose half a dozen White Spot locations to introduce the dish to our guests to get their feedback.

"There are a lot of people tasting our creations," says Chuck. "Most chefs don't get that. With White Spot, you get really good feedback. One of the things that I really strongly believe in, and Mr. Bailey believed in, and the company believes in, is we have to serve a quality product to guests. If the menu item doesn't pass that series of taste tests, then it just doesn't make the menu."

Once guest feedback is reviewed, the dish either gets approved for the menu or is sent back to the kitchen for fine tuning. The whole process takes about a year, which is unique in our industry. "Nobody works a year out," says Danny. We believe that if we want to launch a new hearty stew, for example, we have to create that stew in the winter, and we have to get it to our taste testers while it's still cold out. Nobody wants to eat stew in summer, so if it's not tested in the winter, the test results will be skewed.

Executive Chef Chuck Currie with Melissa Craig (left) at our Tastes Like Spring TV shoot in 2009 and with Pino Posteraro (right) at our Bella Italia TV shoot in 2010.

We also have to do due diligence around food allergies and nutritional requirements. For any menu item that falls under the Heart Smart standard set by the Canadian Heart and Stroke Foundation "the parameters are super strict," says Arlana Alkema, our in-house nutritionist. "If we overdo the sodium, for example, we have to send it back to the lab for retesting."

Our efforts are paying off. These days "we serve over a million guests a month at White Spot," says Danny. "We are making a lot of people happy. But you can't ignore the fact that if you take something off the menu, someone will be upset." At the same time, a lot of our guests are enthusiastic about our ongoing promotional menus, which offer seasonal items for a limited time. "Right now, no other full-service B.C. restaurant chain buys more local products than we do," says Warren. More than 50 per cent of our ingredients are locally sourced, including the 100 per cent fresh Canadian beef for our award-winning burgers, the chicken for our popular chicken dishes, the Kennebec potatoes for our famous fresh-cut fries, the blueberries for our pies, the wild salmon, juicy tomatoes, homegrown mushrooms, creamy ice cream, milk, eggs and the buns for our

Our new West Coast-inspired decor is warm and inviting and features separate lounge areas to enhance the social experience.

burgers, which are baked fresh at a commercial bakery according to our specific, time-tested recipe and ingredients. In 2012, we were also the first restaurant chain in British Columbia to offer a 100 per cent B.C. VQA wine list.

"We are attracting guests who thought they were going to have a burger but then end up having something different," says Danny. "If we continue to be innovative and expand on our menu offerings, we will always have something for everyone. Of course, the classics will always be great sellers. Our burgers remain our most popular menu items by far."

We need to please a wider variety of tastes more than ever, and that's a challenge we're willing to tackle. In the spirit of Nat, we are forever listening to feedback, tweaking our concept and striving to be everything that our guests expect us to be. That may sound like a tall order, but striving for that goal is what keeps us on our toes. In this increasingly competitive marketplace, we don't take any of our success for granted.

Members of our menu development team: Arlana Alkema, James Kennedy, Chuck Currie, Warren Erhart and Danny Markowicz.

Desserts

Berry Shortcake

BERRIES

1 lb strawberries, blueberries, raspberries or blackberries (or any combination of any of them)

¼ cup granulated sugar

BISCUITS

1¼ cups cake flour

1¼ cups all-purpose flour

½ cup + 2 Tbsp granulated sugar

1 Tbsp baking powder

¾ tsp baking soda

¾ tsp kosher salt

¼ lb unsalted butter (½ cup), cold, roughly chopped

1 cup + 3 Tbsp homogenized milk

1½ tsp fresh lemon juice

WHIPPED CREAM

½ cup whipping cream

1½ tsp granulated sugar

½ tsp vanilla extract

FRESH SUMMER BERRIES are magnificent, and the biscuits in this recipe are a perfect complement. We spent two days in the White Spot test kitchen trying different flours and leavening agents to get this biscuit recipe just right.

BERRIES Quarter strawberries if using. Toss berries and sugar in a bowl, then allow to sit, tossing occasionally, for 30 minutes.

BISCUITS Preheat the oven to 375 °F. Line a baking sheet with parchment paper.

In an electric mixer fitted with a paddle attachment, combine flours, 2 Tbsp of the sugar, baking powder, baking soda and salt until well mixed. Add butter and mix until it is in ⅛-inch pieces. With the motor running at low speed, pour in 1 cup of the milk and lemon juice all at once and mix until the dough is just uniform and gathered tightly around the paddle.

Lightly dust a clean work surface with flour and turn the dough onto it. Dust your fingers with flour, then shape the dough into a 6 × 9-inch rectangle. Pat it together well so that the rectangle is uniform, without any cracks it in. Cut dough once lengthwise, then twice widthwise to form 6 biscuits, each 3 inches square. (If you use a round cookie cutter to make biscuits, you have to rework the leftover dough to use it all up, which makes it tough. Just make square biscuits instead!) Arrange the biscuits in a single layer on the baking sheet, leaving 1 inch around each.

In a small bowl, combine the remaining ½ cup sugar and 3 Tbsp milk to make a glaze. Using your fingers, press down on the centre of each biscuit to make a shallow depression in the dough. Spoon glaze into the depressions, then bake biscuits for 20 to 25 minutes until puffed, firm and golden brown.

WHIPPED CREAM Using an electric mixer, beat cream, sugar and vanilla until stiff peaks form.

TO ASSEMBLE Cut open the biscuits and place 2 halves on each plate. Cover the bottom of the biscuit with berries and a dollop of whipped cream, then top with the other half of the biscuit placed at an angle.

Bumbleberry Pie

THIS LOVELY FRUIT pie can be made with blueberries, raspberries, strawberries or blackberries: bumbleberry just means a mixture of any of those!

To wash the berries, place them in a colander and gently rinse them under cold running water for at least 30 seconds. Dry them in a salad spinner lined with paper towels. If you have leftover fresh berries, they will last longer if you clean them with a mixture of one part lemon juice to three parts cold water and then refrigerate them in an airtight container lined with paper towels. Serve this pie with whipped cream or vanilla ice cream.

PASTRY CRUST Using an electric mixer fitted with a paddle attachment, beat butter, sugar and salt on low until smooth. Add egg and mix until just combined, then stir in flour until just blended. Cover and refrigerate until chilled.

Preheat the oven to 400°F. Lightly grease a 9-inch pie tin with cooking spray. Lightly dust a clean work surface with flour. Roll out dough to a thickness of ⅛ inch and place in the pie tin. Bake for about 12 minutes until firm and golden brown. Allow to cool to room temperature.

BUMBLEBERRY FILLING Gently combine the berries in a large bowl until well mixed. In a food processor, purée 2½ cups of the mixed berries. Strain the mixture through a fine-mesh strainer into a bowl, and, using a stiff rubber spatula, push as much of the juices and fine pulp through the strainer as you can. Discard the seeds and pulp from the strainer.

Pour the fruit juice into a nonstick pan. Add sugar, cornstarch, salt, lemon juice and red currant jelly and mix until well combined. Bring just to a simmer on medium heat, remove from the heat and allow to cool for 5 minutes. Place remaining berries in a bowl, add the cooked fruit mixture and mix until well combined.

TO ASSEMBLE Pour the bumbleberry filling into the pastry crust and refrigerate until set, about 15 minutes. Serve chilled, warmed or at room temperature and cut into individual slices.

MAKES ONE 9-INCH PIE

PASTRY CRUST
½ lb unsalted butter (1 cup)
⅜ cup granulated sugar
¼ tsp kosher salt
1 large egg
2⅜ cups pastry flour

BUMBLEBERRY FILLING
2 cups raspberries
2 cups blackberries
2 cups blueberries
½ cup granulated sugar
3 Tbsp cornstarch
⅛ tsp kosher salt
1 Tbsp fresh lemon juice
2 Tbsp red currant jelly

Limoncello Pie

MAKES ONE 9-INCH PIE

½ cup + 2 Tbsp
granulated sugar

¼ cup cornstarch

⅛ tsp kosher salt

5 large egg yolks

1¾ cups homogenized
or 2 per cent milk

½ cup evaporated milk

½ vanilla bean,
about 3 inches long,
split lengthwise

2 Tbsp unsalted butter

3 Tbsp limoncello liqueur

½ cup fresh lemon juice

2 tsp grated lemon zest

Pastry Crust (page 143)

THIS RECIPE WAS developed for our 2010 Bella Italia promotion with Pino Posteraro, owner of Cioppino's Mediterranean Grill and Enoteca, in Vancouver. Just as Nat insisted on quality, Pino often popped into White Spot when we were testing this recipe to make sure it tasted just right. On one visit, the custard in the pie was a little too loose for Pino's liking. He discussed the problem with Chuck, and it was solved. This version is slightly different from the one we served in the restaurant, but it's easier to make at home. Serve with whipped cream.

IN A SAUCEPAN, whisk together sugar, cornstarch and salt on medium heat. Beat in yolks one at a time, then slowly whisk in milks. Add vanilla bean. Cook, stirring frequently at first, then constantly as the mixture begins to simmer and thicken, about 8 minutes. Continue to cook, stirring constantly, for 1 minute more. Remove from the heat, whisk in butter, limoncello liqueur, lemon juice and lemon zest. Remove the vanilla bean and scrape the seeds into the filling. Discard the pod. Pour the filling into a shallow pan, smoothing it out. Place a piece of plastic wrap directly on the surface of the filling to prevent a skin from forming, and allow to cool for 30 minutes at room temperature.

Pour the warm filling into the baked pastry crust. Once again, place a sheet of plastic wrap directly over the filling surface. Refrigerate the pie until completely chilled, at least 3 hours. Slice and serve.

Sticky Toffee
Banana Bread Pudding

BANANA BREAD IS pretty fantastic all by itself, but when you make it into a pudding and add a butterscotch-caramel sauce, it's positively decadent! Make the sauce while the pudding is cooking, then serve it warm over the hot pudding and scoops of French vanilla bean ice cream.

BANANA BREAD PUDDING Preheat the oven to 350°F. Lightly butter and flour a 9 × 5-inch metal loaf pan.

In a medium bowl, whisk flour with baking soda and salt. In another bowl, whisk beaten eggs with canola oil, 1 cup of the sugar and bananas. Stir the banana mixture into the dry ingredients until well combined. Scrape the batter into the loaf pan and bake in the centre of the oven for about 50 minutes, or until golden and a toothpick inserted into the centre of the loaf comes out clean. Remove from the oven, set the pan on a cooling rack and allow to cool for 15 minutes. Turn the bread out onto the rack and allow it to cool completely, about 30 minutes.

Again, preheat the oven to 350°F. Lightly grease a 9 × 9-inch baking pan with cooking spray.

Cut cooled banana bread into ¾- to 1-inch cubes, arrange them on a baking sheet and bake for 6 to 8 minutes until lightly toasted. Turn down the oven to 325°F.

In a large bowl, whisk the 8 eggs well, then whisk in milk, cream, the remaining 6 Tbsp sugar and vanilla. Using a spatula, gently fold in banana bread and pour the pudding mixture into the baking pan. Bake for about 45 minutes, or until the centre of the pudding springs back when pressed. (The internal temperature of the pudding should be 170°F.)

BUTTERSCOTCH-CARAMEL SAUCE In a small saucepan, bring sugar, butter and cream to a boil on medium-high heat, stirring constantly. Immediately remove from the heat and allow to cool slightly.

TO ASSEMBLE Slice pudding into squares or 1-inch slices and arrange on individual plates. Drizzle with warm butterscotch-caramel sauce and serve immediately.

SERVES 6

BANANA BREAD PUDDING
Butter for greasing loaf pan

1¼ cups all-purpose flour + more for dusting the loaf pan

1 tsp baking soda

Pinch of salt

2 large eggs, beaten

½ cup canola oil

1 cup + 6 Tbsp granulated sugar

2 large, very ripe bananas, mashed

8 large eggs

2 cups milk

2 cups whipping cream

1 tsp vanilla extract

BUTTERSCOTCH-CARAMEL SAUCE
1½ cups brown sugar

¼ lb butter (½ cup), in small pieces

½ cup whipping cream

Apple Pie

MAKES ONE 9-INCH PIE

SHORT-DOUGH CRUST

6 Tbsp butter, room temperature + more for greasing the pie tin

6 Tbsp granulated sugar

½ beaten large egg

¾ tsp vanilla extract

1¼ cups all-purpose flour + more for dusting the pie tin

1¼ tsp baking powder

ALMOND-OATMEAL TOPPING

3 Tbsp sliced toasted almonds

¾ cup rolled oats

½ cup all-purpose flour

½ cup brown sugar

¼ tsp cinnamon

⅓ cup melted butter

APPLE FILLING

6 Granny Smith apples, peeled, cored and cut in ¼-inch slices (3 cups)

1½ cups brown sugar

¾ cup whipping cream

3 Tbsp + 1 tsp fresh lemon juice

½ tsp cinnamon

5 Tbsp + 1 tsp cornstarch

THIS IS A really impressive pie that will have your family and friends' jaws dropping. It is made with a simple short-dough crust that you don't even have to roll—you can press it into a pie tin or plate instead! Serve with ice cream or whipped cream or slices of aged cheddar cheese.

CRUST Lightly butter a 9-inch pie tin and dust it with flour.

In an electric mixer fitted with a paddle attachment, beat butter and sugar until fluffy. Add egg and vanilla and beat until smooth. In a small bowl, combine flour and baking powder, then add to the butter mixture and beat until uniform and sticky. Dust your fingers with flour, then press the dough evenly into the pie tin, about ¼ inch deep, until it is nice and even. (You may need to dip your fingers in flour a few times to do this, as the short dough is quite sticky.) Set aside.

ALMOND-OATMEAL TOPPING In a medium bowl, combine all the ingredients until well mixed.

APPLE FILLING In a large bowl, toss apples and brown sugar until well coated. Pour the mixture into a colander and set it over the bowl for 45 minutes to allow apples to absorb the sugar and release some of their juices into the bowl.

In a large nonstick frying pan, combine the juice from the apples with cream, lemon juice, cinnamon and cornstarch on medium heat. Bring to a simmer, then remove from the heat and fold in apples using a rubber spatula. As the apple mixture cools, toss it gently but thoroughly with your hands.

TO ASSEMBLE Preheat the oven to 300 °F. Firmly press the apple filling into the short-dough crust, piling it into a really nice high mound. Press the topping into the apple filling. Bake for about 1½ hours, or until topping is dark golden brown and apples are just soft but fully cooked. Allow to cool to room temperature before cutting. Serve warmed and cut into individual slices.

Beyond B.C.'s Borders

NAT HAD AN eye to the future, and as an innovative entrepreneur he was devoted to growing the concept that he believed in. We are carrying the torch for Nat as we continue to expand his B.C. tradition for great food, great service and raving fans into markets nowhere close to Nat's old stomping grounds.

If Nat were here today, he'd be incredibly proud to see what we have planned for a business that began so humbly, out of a BBQ chicken shack in the undeveloped outback of old Vancouver. In the last three decades, we've gone from 27 locations to 125 White Spots and Triple-O's, including our presence on major B.C. Ferries routes. There are 61 full-service White Spots in B.C. and 4 in Alberta. There are 53 Triple-O's in B.C. and Alberta. And our 30-foot Triple-O's "on the go" mobile food truck has taken our burgers, fries and milkshakes to the streets and to corporate, community and charitable events.

With the commitment of our franchisees, we have six Triple-O's in Hong Kong, two in mainland China and three in Singapore, and in 2013, we are opening yet another Triple-O's in Singapore as well as our first in the Philippines. That's just the start.

In the next three years, White Spot will undergo major expansion throughout Western Canada. We'll then move farther east, to bring the great taste of White Spot to Ontario, where we already know there's big demand for our burgers from former British Columbians who've moved east for work.

Today, B.C.'s own Toigo family continues what Nat set out to do, which is grow the restaurant according to the needs of our guests by moving into new markets, updating our menu items, continuing to

At Home with the Bublés

BEING A Burnaby boy, singer Michael Bublé has been a White Spot regular all his life. Though he travels worldwide, that doesn't stop him from eating at White Spot. He's even got his Argentinean wife, Luisana Lopilato, and her entire family hooked on our food. When the couple arrives home in Vancouver, they stop at White Spot before they even go home to unpack. "Literally, we don't even drop our bags at home. We stop at White Spot and get the hamburgers. Lu loves her Double Doubles. And she loves the Zoo Sticks.

"And one of her favourite things to do on date night, my wife—because they don't have it in Argentina—she loves to take the car and get the carhop service. Of all the things you can go and do in beautiful Vancouver, my wife loves to go to the West Van White Spot carhop service. They know us pretty well there."

And, of course, with Michael being the family-centric guy he is, White Spot has a place in the hearts of the Bublé clan, too. "I take my grandparents to the one at Lougheed and Gilmore. That's the one we would go to when we were kids," says Michael. "My grandpa did the plumbing there. It's still such a part of my life—it really is."

source ingredients locally and maintaining our position as Canada's longest-running restaurant chain success story.

"My father would be pleased," says Ron. "He'd feel good about the way things have turned out. He did all the heavy lifting, and he created this asset. One of our biggest strengths is we hire the best people we can and we support them when we can, and then we get out of their way. We have maintained that. Restaurants are a people business."

Adds Peter Jr., "We are working on the same principles as my father believed in—as in, how to run a business. You just have to outdo the rest of the competition out there. You must have the best service, the best-tasting food, the freshest food, and you have to execute it consistently. To take your family to White Spot costs a lot less than you'd spend at one of the other major chains, and our guests expect that. You have to be on top of it all the time. There is no rest. It's about service. The guest is always first. You have to look after your guests.

"And you have to listen—and if you do that, you won't be out of touch. There's a reason our company has been around since 1928." Nat would be proud!

Metric Conversions

(rounded off to the nearest whole number)

Weight

Imperial or U.S.	Metric
1 oz	30 g
2 oz	60 g
3 oz	85 g
4 oz (¼ lb)	115 g
5 oz	140 g
6 oz	170 g
7 oz	200 g
8 oz (½ lb)	225 g
9 oz	255 g
10 oz	285 g
11 oz	310 g
12 oz (¾ lb)	340 g
13 oz	370 g
14 oz	400 g
15 oz	425 g
16 oz (1 lb)	455 g
2 lbs	910 g

Volume

Imperial or U.S.	Metric
⅛ tsp	0.5 mL
¼ tsp	1 mL
½ tsp	2.5 mL
¾ tsp	4 mL
1 tsp	5 mL
1 Tbsp	15 mL
1½ Tbsp	23 mL
⅛ cup	30 mL
¼ cup	60 mL
⅓ cup	80 mL
½ cup	120 mL
⅔ cup	160 mL
¾ cup	180 mL
1 cup	240 mL

Liquid Measures

Imperial or U.S.	Metric
1 fl oz	30 mL
1½ fl oz	45 mL
2 fl oz	60 mL
3 fl oz	90 mL
4 fl oz	120 mL

Oven Temperature

Imperial or U.S.	Metric
165°F	75°C
170°F	77°C
275°F	135°C
300°F	150°C
325°F	160°C
350°F	180°C
375°F	190°C
400°F	200°C
425°F	220°C
450°F	230°C

Linear

Imperial or U.S.	Metric
⅛ inch	3 mm
¼ inch	6 mm
½ inch	12 mm
¾ inch	2 cm
1 inch	2.5 cm
1¼ inches	3 cm
1½ inches	3.5 cm
1¾ inches	4.5 cm
2 inches	5 cm
3 inches	7.5 cm
4 inches	10 cm
5 inches	12.5 cm
6 inches	15 cm
7 inches	18 cm
12 inches	30 cm
24 inches	60 cm

Baking utensils

Imperial or U.S.	Metric
9 × 5-inch loaf pan	2 L loaf pan
9 × 9-inch baking pan	22.5 × 22.5-cm baking pan

Acknowledgements

WHITE SPOT WOULD like to extend a special thank you to the following individuals from our Home Office for their tireless efforts and determination to make our first cookbook a reality:

Arlana Alkema, Menu Development
Kathryn Quick, Marketing Manager
Cathy Tostenson, Vice President, Marketing & Menu Development

White Spot would like to acknowledge the following staff and management who provided their generous assistance with this project:

Denise Buchanan, Vice President, Human Resources
Liz Cool, Design & Construction Administrative Assistant
Chuck Currie, Executive Chef
Warren Erhart, President & CEO
Talisa Hebert, Red Seal Chef
Al Hewlett, Server
Kim Hewlett, Hostess
James Kennedy, Corporate Training Chef
Nelia Laguyan, Red Seal Apprentice Level 2
Danny Markowicz, Executive Development Chef
Verni Niles, Red Seal Apprentice Level 2
Peter Toigo Jr., Managing Director, Shato Holdings
Ron Toigo, Managing Director, Shato Holdings
Peter Yang, Red Seal Chef

White Spot would like to thank the following individuals for their contributions to this project:

Bruce Allen
Mark Andrews
John Bishop
Michael Bublé
Wayne Cox
Melissa Craig
David Foster
Michael J. Fox
Peter Guichon
Erwin Jellen

Frank Leone
Len Leroux
Michele Metcalfe-Kletke
Jim Pattison
Pino Posteraro
Pat Quinn
Red Robinson
Joe Scianna
Dale Vaux

Index